Marcus Aurelius Updated:
21st Century Meditations
On Living Life

Kelvin H. Chin

Marcus Aurelius Updated: 21st Century Meditations On Living Life
Kelvin H. Chin

Copyright © 2021 Kelvin H. Chin

For permission requests, please contact the author at www.KelvinChin.org

Published in the United States by Aurelian Press.

ISBN 978-0-9977174-1-9

Jacket design: Sam "Wilhelmine" Chin
Interior design: Susan Veach
Book Manager: Kathryn Bartman

To all seekers of truth, virtue,
knowledge & happiness

*"Humans have come into being for
the sake of each other;
so teach them or learn to bear them."*

— Marcus Aurelius

CONTENTS

Chapter 1 — My Favorite Marcus Aurelius Meditations

Chapter 2 — Emotions

Chapter 3 — Life Principles

Chapter 4 — Meditation

Chapter 5 — The Spiritual

ACKNOWLEDGMENTS

This book is dedicated to my father Henry W.F. Chin and my mother King C.L. Chin.

To my father this lifetime, Henry, who taught me patience and the inescapability of Free Will with his unchanging views on all things in life, including that his mind would not continue after he died, until he was surprised. And, especially to my 20th century mother King who demonstrated to me through her indomitable spirit in her 5'0" frame what a Renaissance woman could accomplish in her abbreviated life, and her constant encouragement to think and act "out of the box," starting with her suggestion that I memorize Alfred Lord Tennyson's "Charge of the Light Brigade" to fulfill a second-grade poetry recitation assignment.

Special heartfelt thanks to my friends who have given invaluable input on this collection of essays — George Hammond, Greg Berning, Kamin Lambertson, Matt Frank, Annmarie Martin and William Baldridge. To my daughter Sam for her artistic talents in designing the book cover. And to both of my gifted and loving children Jesse Abbott Chin and Samantha Chin, who remind me through their presence in my life the importance of living life fully now in the continual present.

Finally, I am especially grateful to my book manager, Kathryn Bartman, for her assistance in the preparation of this book for publication.

INTRODUCTION

The Roman emperor Marcus Aurelius wrote what are today known as his "Meditations" as daily reflections upon various ideas and concepts concerning life and the pursuit of happiness. He often wrote them in quiet moments while in a Roman fort or in his tent between battlefield campaigns far from Rome. He did not write them expecting they would be published. He wrote them for himself — as a method of refining his thoughts on living life, as a way to promote his continual endeavor of self-teaching and self-development.

Sixteen centuries later, Frederick the Great of Prussia "modeled his life after Marcus." He even sought out, and bought at great price, a superb Roman statue sculpted during Marcus's lifetime and had it prominently placed in a wooded grove at his favorite palace, *Sans Souci*, in Potsdam near Berlin.

Neither man wanted the role of ruler. Marcus hated having to move into Hadrian's palace for further grooming to be emperor. And Frederick even more boldly tried to escape to England when he was a young prince at age 18. But both men nevertheless took on the challenges of the role and governed their people as successful leaders, always viewing themselves as the "trustee in the service of his people," never there for personal gain.

Sharing Marcus's deep interest in Stoic philosophy, Frederick often wrote about ancient Roman ideals, and regularly convened a group of 11 close friends to discuss various issues including the art of war, the ideas and moods of the times, music, and philosophy. The 12 of them called themselves "The Bayard

Order," and each had a different symbolic pseudonym. And instead of calling Frederick's first palace Rheinsberg, they called it "Remusberg."

This was Frederick's nod to the founding story of Rome about the twin brothers Romulus and Remus. Remus was killed by his brother in a fraternal feud, so it seemed only fitting that Frederick and his friends would name their meeting place in Prussia — to them, a symbolic "Rome" where they would discuss Marcus's and other ancient Roman and Greek philosophers' ideas — after Remus. That was Frederick's way of bestowing on the slain brother the honor that Remus had missed out on 2500 years earlier.

Similarly, I have written these essays over the past several years quite spontaneously, as the ideas bubbled up in my consciousness, and as tools to help my students and myself as we each navigate life in our respective attempts to "live a good life," a happy life. I did not write them expecting to publish them in book form — that idea came later.

These essays were not written originally in any particular order (that also came later), but simply, as I said, as they occurred to me at that moment in my life — sometimes inspired due to the circumstances of that day, other times spurred by questions that came up from some of you, my students.

And when I say "students" I mean that in the most inclusive sense — some of you may have been my formal students in my classes, while others may have interacted with me at a conference or in a podcast, or even during a private phone session. All of your questions have contributed to my delving deeper within to explore my own thinking and perspectives on the topics in this book.

In a sense, therefore, many of you have contributed to this collection of essays. And for your involvement — whether conscious or not — I thank you.

THEMES

There are certain themes running thr⟨ough⟩ Aurelius's "Meditations" from the 2nd ce⟨ntury⟩ the themes are timeless — as applicable in 11⟨...⟩ as they were in 170 A.D. After he acknowledg⟨es⟩ what he has learned from the key influence⟨s —⟩ his grandparents, parents, adoptive father, ⟨...⟩ and teachers in his youth — Marcus launche⟨s⟩ philosophical maxims expressing his ideas and ⟨a⟩ range of subjects.

Some of the main themes are how to enjo⟨y a⟩ productive life; how to live a life without eith⟨er⟩ people or what he refers to as "Nature," as a wh⟨ole;⟩ more clearly, using one's access to "Reason" a⟨nd⟩ more effectively; the value of going within ⟨and⟩ seeking answers to life and for being more me⟨...⟩ how to be a more spiritual being, living in harm⟨ony⟩ how to nurture one's relations with "the gods" (⟨...⟩ and Roman belief system); and how to overc⟨ome⟩ death so that it does not prevent one from livin⟨g.⟩

In my book, you will see similar themes. ⟨...⟩ have written a separate book on *Overcoming t⟨...⟩* already, I have not included essays I have writte⟨n⟩ in this book.

I have organized these essays into the fol⟨lowing⟩ sections: Emotions, Life Principles, Meditation, ⟨...⟩ One vocabulary note: I use the term "mind" a⟨s⟩

co⟨...⟩
wo⟨...⟩
or ⟨...⟩
cul⟨...⟩

Au⟨...⟩
ide⟨...⟩
co⟨...⟩
of ⟨...⟩

sciousness, soul, spirit, etc. I use "mind" like this because I
k with people from all belief systems — whether religious
ultural — in 45 countries so far. So I use language that is as
urally neutral as possible.

Since this book was inspired by my resonance with Marcus
elius's approach and perspectives on various life-affirming
s, I will start with my favorite Marcus "meditations" and my
iments on each, as a jumping off point for this compilation
1st century essays.

Chapter 1

MY FAVORITE MARCUS AURELIUS MEDITATIONS

2.14 — Living in the Present*

"Even if you should live three thousand years, or thirty thousand for that matter, know just the same that no one loses any other life than the one he now lives, nor does one live any other life than that which he will lose. The longest and shortest lives thus amount to the same, for the present moment is equal for everyone, and what we lose turns out never to have belonged to us in the first place; and so what has been lost is only a mere moment. Nobody can lose either the past or the future, for how can anyone lose what they never possessed?"

Marcus is reminding us to "live in the present." That it is futile and an utter waste of energy to live in either the past or the future — although many of us do just that. I call it the illusion of living emotionally "beyond the imagination horizon," i.e., the future. It is an illusion because the reality is that each of us always is living in the "continual present." The "continual" present because the present is ever-changing in the following way. What you read a word (never mind a sentence) ago is now your "past" because you are — like all of us — always living in the continual present. Now this is the present, now this, now this, etc.

Moreover, Marcus implicitly reminds us that whether you believe you will live many other lifetimes for thousands of years, or just one lifetime — and whether life is long or short — that we each possess the "now," that present in which to live it, moment to moment. So, we should not waste time worrying about losing it — or anything associated with it — for that too is an illusion, because what turns out to have been lost is merely that present moment, which is now the past. In the end, his is a practical reminder to us to live now, in the moment with ourselves and those we love.

---

* These Marcus Aurelius quotations are numbered and translated by Jacob Needleman & John P. Piazza, *The Essential Marcus Aurelius* (2008).

4.3 — Turning Within

"People seek retreats for themselves in the country, by the sea, and near the mountains; and you too are especially prone to desire such things. But this is a sign of ignorance, since you have the power to retire within yourself whenever you wish. For nowhere can a person retire more full of peace and free from care than into one's own soul; above all, if one has that place within oneself into which one can turn one's attention, one is immediately at ease. And by ease I mean nothing other than the right ordering of the whole person. Continually give yourself this kind of retreat and regenerate yourself, but keep your rules of living brief and basic so that, when consulted, they will immediately wash away all distress and send you back to your work without resentment."

Marcus tells us we do not have to escape to the Isle of Capri, or Nepal, or a cabin in Big Bear to relax. We can relax wherever we are. Because all we need to do is close our eyes and "turn within," as I call it. And as he says, it can be done easily and effortlessly — "keeping the rules brief and basic." It is not complicated. And by doing this easy process on a regular basis, we develop a more clear-thinking and peaceful mind — which in turn, recharges our internal batteries, and our energy is rejuvenated. And then, we are ready to reengage with our daily lives free from stress, embracing life more fully than before, seamlessly — "without resentment."

4.3 — Balance & Perspective

"...Remember the humble refuge which is yourself. And, above all, do not be anxious or overextend yourself, but be truly independent....But among the thoughts that are closest at hand, which you will look to, let these two be there: first, that various difficulties need not penetrate to your soul but can remain

external, unaffecting – such disturbances come from nothing
other than your internal judgments; second, remember that all
the things which you now see are changing and will not continue
to exist as they are. Continually bear in mind how many changes
you have already witnessed. The Cosmos is constant change, and
our lives are but a series of choices."

Marcus encourages us again to look inside. To "turn within," to "Know Thyself," to gain greater self-knowledge. And by doing so, we will gain greater balance and perspective in life. He describes what I often reframe as "we are not our thoughts, they are external to who we are. We are the experiencer of our experiences. We are not the experiences that we have." And so in that sense, they do not really affect "who we are," they do not change our identity. That any such influence or power over us is something we project onto those thoughts ourselves — what Marcus calls "your internal judgment." His second point is to highlight the fact that each of us makes continual choices in life, and that all of that is part of the constantly changing nature of experiences and events that occur throughout our individual lives, as well as the universe. We each have Free Will, exercised as a series of choices. By seeing life in this light, we gain greater balance and perspective. And thus, more happiness and freedom.

5.20 — Free Will

"From one point of view, every human being is closely connected
to us; therefore all people must be treated well and tolerated. But
from another point of view, insofar as any human stands in the
way of actions which are my proper duty, then mankind becomes
just another one of all the things which are not my concern, no
less than the sun or the wind or a wild animal. Though my action
could be hindered by one of these, my motivation and state of

mind cannot be hindered, thanks to my ability to :
adapt to any circumstance. For the mind can conv
hinders its activity into things which help it, all th
work into assistance in that very task, and all that
path into an escort on its journey."

Marcus again emphasizes his reminder to
us that we each exercise our individual Free W
own personal choices throughout our lives. H
are all connected to one another in some wa
community, and as such we should treat each ot
However, if someone (or some situation) stands
your accomplishing your objectives in life, the
absolute barrier. We each can always find a wa
wise, judicious, practical and effective choice
circumstance — to get our objective met. Yes,
back and say, "Woe is me, I have run up against
Or, as Marcus suggests, we can instead think
find ways to convert the energy or situation tha
into something that propels us forward in our j
accomplishing our objective.

Most Americans, and many people worldw
Brady's story. In 2000, he was the 199th draft p
round of the NFL draft and was finally signed by t
Patriots football team in my home state of Mass;
NFL teams passed on Brady. He currently has
six Super Bowl rings, one for every quarterbac
of him in 2000. It is well known that Brady has
people would view as that "barrier," as his very
of self-motivation. He converted that publicl
assessment of his potential — at least by others
his unparalleled success on the playing field. B
sat back, felt sorry for himself for being picke

ft, taken his $193,000 rookie salary, sulked on the bench ind their starting QB Drew Bledsoe, and quit after a year to sell life insurance (he is on record saying that is what he might e ended up doing if he had not been drafted by the Patriots). t he didn't.

It is our Free Will and creativity that we each can access and : to be successful in our lives. We need to exercise it. Like Tom dy did.

37 — Free Will & Destiny

*here was a time, long past, when fate was kind to me.' [a
nmon tragic lament from the 2nd century] But the truly
tunate person has created his own good fortune through good
its of the soul, good intentions, and good actions."*

Marcus is talking about Free Will and Destiny (Fate) in this xim. We each have the free will to do whatever we choose — have personal choice. And based on those choices, certain sequences to our thoughts and actions follow. There is no h thing as "absolute" destiny, or fate. Everything is subject to nge depending on the choices we make. And here, Marcus n breaks it down more subtly for us by suggesting that it starts per within us in our "soul" or consciousness — at that more tract level within each of us, what I call "how connected within selves we are with our own minds." Then to the intentional el which is a less abstract, more concrete manifestation of our nking process, which in turn manifests in our actions based those choices our mind makes from among those intentions d thoughts. So, essentially he is saying: Don't wallow in self- y as described in that ancient adage about Fate not being kind you. Instead, take control of your life from the inside out. ke good choices and you can create your own good fortune.

"Fate" does not control your fortune. You do. We each create our own destinies, our own futures.

6.11 — Happiness

"Whenever you are forced by circumstances to be disturbed in some way, quickly return to yourself, and do not lose your footing any longer than is absolutely necessary; for you will have more control over your internal harmony by continually returning to it."

Marcus is saying the way to happiness is to start on the inside. I call it the "inside-out approach." By taking that approach, no matter what the external disturbance might be, it will not overwhelm us, and therefore we will not get stressed and unhappy from it. That is where true "control" and "internal harmony" comes from — inside each of us — not by controlling things outside of us.

6.21 — Knowledge

"If someone is able to show me that what I think or do is not right, I will happily change, for I seek the truth, by which no one ever was truly harmed. Harmed is the person who continues in his self-deception and ignorance."

The pursuit of knowledge ("truth") is not static. It is a fluid process. We constantly need to question our assumptions and interpretations against the yardsticks of common sense, logic, and consistency. There is no such thing as perfection, because that implies a static, non-changing state. And that simply does not exist, since we are forever growing, learning more about ourselves and the universe around us. Moreover, continuing to expand and refine our knowledge about ourselves is imperative to manifesting a fruitful, happy and productive life. Conversely, by being stubborn and getting stuck in our ways, and continuing to make false assumptions — or to think irrationally or inconsistently — will lead to poor decisions and thus, unhappiness. This is what Marcus refers to as "harming" oneself by continuing down the path of "self-deception and ignorance."

6.44 — Gods & Angels

"If the gods have made decisions concerning me, in particular what must happen to me, no doubt they have made good decisions, for not easily could one conceive of a god who is lacking in wisdom... however, if it is indeed the case that they do not make decisions concerning my interests, it nevertheless remains within my power to make decisions concerning myself. My search is for what is beneficial. The benefit for each is in accordance with how they are made and their specific nature, and my nature pertains both to Reason and to society. My city is Rome, insofar as I am Antoninus; but insofar as I am a human being, my city is the Cosmos. Therefore all that benefits these cities is alone my good."

Marcus is pointing out that even though he believes in the gods, and that the gods most likely have his best interests in their minds, even if they make mistakes about his interests, it always remains in *his* power to make different decisions that *are* in his personal interest. As I often remind us, we are each responsible for ourselves. No one else is responsible for our thoughts and actions — not our spouse, not our children, not our teachers, and not our gods, angels or other beings we may revere. At the end of the day, each of us must listen to ourselves first. Not blindly follow what others — even the gods or angels — might tell us. We should always use our common sense, our reasoning mind.

In his last statement about Rome and the Cosmos, he is

saying that the "society" to which he belongs is not just the city of Rome, but also includes the greater universe as a whole in which he is a human being like everyone else, not an emperor. And that he sees it as his responsibility — in his "nature" — to see to it that everything he does benefits those two "cities" — Rome and the vast Cosmos, in which Earth is just a small part. This underscores Marcus's view of himself as one of many individuals in the universe, no more or less important than any other, and nevertheless cognizant of his personal responsibility in both his citizenships — of Rome and the Cosmos — to do his best to promote his own well-being, as well as the well-being of others.

7.59 — Meditation, Turning Within

"Turn your attention within for the fountain of all that is good lies within, and it is always ready to pour forth, if you continually delve in."

"Turning within" is the key to self-knowledge. Closing one's eyes to meditate is a critical component to daily life in order for us to tap into that reservoir within each of us that helps us release our stresses, restore inner balance, and connect with our essential nature, i.e., the vastness of our minds. And as Marcus reminds us, we take our minds wherever we go! It is always there, and always readily available to sustain us.

7.65 — Cruelty & The Importance of Being Important

"See that you never feel toward the inhumane what they feel toward humankind."

Marcus is speaking about cruelty and what I call the

"Importance of Being Important." As you can see, it has been a fundamental problem of the human race for many thousands of years. We see it daily — played out in our politics, business, and all levels of our society. Just as Marcus saw it 2,000 years ago.

But what is he shining a light on with respect to cruelty? What subtle point is he making here in this very short maxim? Marcus is telling us that exercising cruelty on the cruel only makes the cruel person *even more cruel*. It does not make the cruel person less cruel. In fact the best way to rehabilitate a cruel person is to shower them with education, understanding, and love. Because that is what they have been missing in their life. Intellectual and emotional support to give them higher self-esteem and more self-confidence. That is why they have resorted to being cruel — to make themselves feel more important than others around them by making those people feel subservient and fearful of them. By lowering the confidence level of those around them, the bully (the "inhumane") feels stronger. Marcus succinctly tells us that being inhumane to the inhumane is not the right way either to reform them or to minimize their impact on you.

7.69 — Fulfillment

"Fulfillment of one's character is the attainment of this: to live each day as if it were the last; to be neither agitated nor numb; and never to act with pretense."

Happiness is achieved when one lives more fully in the moment, in the continual present — not just physically, but also mentally, emotionally. It arises from a state of equanimity that resides at neither extreme — not angrily stressed out, nor robotically emotionless. Living in and acting from a state of inner peace does not mean passivity or lack of passion. Finally, as I often point out, fulfillment also includes living from a state of humility — which can mean from a state of sincere and profound self-confidence, yet without a hint of arrogance.

7.71 — Control

"It is ridiculous to renounce the wickedness of others, which is impossible, rather than renounce one's own wickedness, which is possible."

One of my favorite pieces of advice is to control what you can control, and let go of what you cannot. We cannot "give up" the bad behavior of others — their behavior is out of our control. Only they can change their behavior. But we *can* change our own bad behavior. That is within our control. So that is where we should focus our energies.

7.73 — Happiness & Rewards

"When you have done a good act and another has fared well by it, why seek a third reward besides these, as fools do, be it the reputation for having done a good act or getting something in return?"

Where does our happiness come from? Does it come from outside of us — the things we do, the praise we get, the trophies we collect? Or does it come from inside us — the simple pleasure of knowing we did something productive in and of itself, or maybe that we were helpful to another person — gave an incoming shopper our cart along with a smile or a gentle nod as we exited the supermarket perhaps. Why do we need the Community Service Award, even if we have performed numerous such acts? Why do we need the bumper stickers that tell the outside world how smart our children are? Is that a "smart" way to educate our children — implicitly teaching them that fame and recognition is why you do things in life? That showing off "how much more important (smart) you are than others" is a sign of success?

Marcus would say no, that is not how we should educate our youth. Instead we should teach our children that they do not develop self-esteem from external adulation — bumper stickers and awards — that it comes from within oneself. And we should demonstrate that lesson by our behavior as parents towards our children, boosting their self-worth by building them up from within through our parental praise and loving support, not by buying them more stuff to reward them for merely doing a good deed for others. Marcus would say you should not get rewarded for doing what you should be doing anyway, being a good person. Being a good person is sufficient reward in and of itself to the person who matters, oneself.

8.8 — Knowledge and Compassion Come From Within

"No time to read or study. But it is possible to restrain my pride; it is possible to rise above pleasures and pains; it is possible to rise above reputation; it is possible not only not to be angry with the insensitive and ungrateful but even to care for them."

Marcus is saying, okay, so you don't have time to spend hours on philosophy — or taking workshops. There is no need to do that because true knowledge does not come from books or classes. It comes from within ourselves, from our minds. All we have to do is make a few simple mental shifts in our perspective and take a different approach.

Marcus is telling us that knowledge is from within, and that we already have it — we just need to use the power of our mind and direct it accordingly. And by making these shifts, this will have a huge effect outwardly in our daily lives. We can rise above the limitations he lists, not be constrained and not have our life-force contracted or drained by them. We can even shift from anger to compassion by changing our attitude towards others, our perspective on how we view them — perhaps by seeing what life challenges have caused them to be insensitive and ungrateful, and in that way "care" for them, thereby helping to loosen the negative grip of those influences on them.

8.33 — Balance & Inner Contentment

"Receive without conceit; release without a struggle."

When we come from a place of inner contentment, we can receive praise, gifts and love from others without self-aggrandizement, or in regular lingo, "without getting too big for your britches." With emotional evenness and humility. And in the same way, when it comes time to let go of what has now become old, no longer necessary, or perhaps was never necessary, we can release that without regret or resistance. That is the sign of an inwardly balanced, contented person. One who has found peace within oneself, in the realization that things come and go as part of the flow of life.

8.48 — The Power of the Mind

"Remember that the ruling part of the self becomes unconquerable when it collects itself and is contented with itself, doing nothing it does not will, even if the stand it takes is unreasonable. How much more, then, when it judges with reason and considers all sides of a matter? Thus the mind which is free from disturbance is a citadel of refuge, for humans have nothing

stronger in which they can find refuge and remain uncaptured. Whoever has not seen this is ignorant; whoever has seen this and does not seek refuge is doomed."

Our minds are powerful. Especially when we exercise our rational, logical, common sense part of our mind — what Marcus calls "reason" — and combine that with thinking about an issue from all angles. Such a mind is a fortress, strong from the foundation up through its walls, unshakeable and confident. Marcus alerts us to the fact that not only is this important to see in ourselves as a path to a productive and happy life, but he also cautions that those who see this — yet ignore this — are then knowingly and inevitably creating a life of unhappiness for themselves.

8.51 — Turning Within, Peace & Freedom

"Do not be sloppy in your actions; in conversation, do not be dragged into confusion; and do not allow your thoughts to wander aimlessly. Do not allow your soul either to contract or inflate; and in your external life, do not be overly busy. 'But they kill us, hack us to pieces, and pursue us with curses.' What does any of this have to do with keeping your thought pure, composed, restrained, and just? It is as if someone standing by a fountain of pure and sweet water were to yell curses at it, yet the fountain never stops bubbling with fresh water. Even if you should hurl mud or even throw shit into it, the water will quickly disperse it and wash it away, and in no way be defiled. How, then, can you have such a fountain within yourself? By guarding your freedom each and every hour with kindness, simplicity, and self-respect."

To maintain a state of equanimity and thus freedom from all the confusion, imbalancing influences, and negativity in the world around us, we need to remember that the solution starts within — that it comes from our own inner strength. That we each are like a powerful fountain of clean, pure water flowing forever. And that nothing, unless we allow it to, can disrupt that flow — as long as we maintain our kindness, simplicity and self-respect. And naturally maintaining that balance, in my experience, is enhanced through a regular practice of "turning within."

10.16 — Action

"Stop philosophizing about what a good man is and be one."

Actions speak louder than words. Don't just think about how to improve our lives — take actions that create that state of being. Make it a living reality. Not merely a thought, a hope, or a dream.

10.27 — History as Teacher

"Continually be mindful of how everything that happens now has also happened in previous times and will happen in the future. And place before your eyes all the dramas and stage-sets, which you have learned either from experience or from older accounts, such as the royal court of Hadrian, of Antoninus, of Philip, Alexander, and Croesus — for those were the same dramas as we see now; only the actors are different."

We need to pay attention to history — study it and learn from it. Because while the players may be different human beings acting out the range of human behavior *in different* centuries or cultures, the behavior is the same. Only then can we begin to truly improve our lot as a human species.

Otherwise, we will continue to make the same behavioral blunders over and over again for millennia. Falling into the same behavioral patterns often meeting the same imbalanced, selfish, non-communal objectives repeatedly — generation after generation. This was good advice 2,000 years ago, and it is as valuable today as it was then.

12.4 — Self-Love

"I have often been amazed at how every person loves himself more than he loves others yet places less value on his own judgment of himself than on the judgments of others concerning him.... This shows us that what others think of us counts more for us than our own estimation of ourselves."

What we think of ourselves is what matters most. After all, if we don't love ourselves first, how shaky is our foundation within? Yet so many of us are excessively concerned with "what others think about us." As Marcus showcases this illogical point, it makes no sense. We love ourselves, yet we don't exhibit that love consistently — we are too quick to dispense with that self-love and replace it with self-loathing, if someone else judges us that way. This is a surefire way to unhappiness in life. To regain that foundation within, we must place our self-love and self-respect first, above how others think of us.

12.9 — The Mind is Self-Sufficient

"In the application of principles, you must be like the boxer, not the gladiator, for the latter must put down and take up his weapon, while the boxer has his hand with him always and need only make a fist."

If you know the principles, the technique of "turning within" and applying the appropriate rules, then that is all that is needed. Because the mind is self-sufficient. We take it wherever we go — it is always with us, guaranteed. So, we are like the boxer who only needs to make a fist and he can fight. We simply can close our eyes and turn within. Whereas those who need to have trappings — candles, incense, rituals, robes — are like the gladiator. Because they must have all the accoutrements before they can apply their "principles" — thus, they are at a disadvantage.

Chapter 2

EMOTIONS

Success, Winning & Happiness

Where does happiness come from?

Let's just start with the easy answer that I think most people who've given any thought to this subject have agreed upon...that it comes "from inside."

Sure, there are still many people on the planet who believe that they will be happier if they buy more things, own more fancy clothes, cars, anything with a price tag. There are many who still take a very materialistic view towards happiness — that they can "buy happiness."

But there is increasing awareness that this is a myth, that no matter how much "stuff" you own, you can still be very unhappy.

So, let's just start this discussion by agreeing among ourselves that happiness comes from inside, not from our external world.

OK, now that's out of the way.

But if we dig deeper, let's look at how we really think and feel, if we are honest with ourselves. Let's "turn within" and reflect to see if we can learn a little bit more about ourselves, and perhaps increase our ability to be happier.

After all, the pursuit of happiness is what life is all about, isn't it?

Have you ever tried to help someone, only to find that they were either unreceptive to your advice, or unable to act on it for any number of reasons, leaving you bummed out when that happened? I think all of us have experienced this at least once (more likely, many times) in our lives.

I think it may be helpful for us to ask ourselves — "Where are we drawing our happiness from in that experience?"

The obvious answer is that our happiness is coming from whether or not they follow our advice. Because if they do, then we think they will be happier, and *our* goal of helping them be happier will have been attained.

We will have succeeded.

Our happiness is dependent on *their* happiness. Or at the very least, our happiness is dependent on their listening to us and following our advice.

And we often think that if they are *not* listening to us, then we need to be more persuasive. We need to come up with better arguments to convince them. Or we may need to exert more effort, speak more forcefully, maybe even louder. But does that work?

Sometimes it may seem to work, they may actually start to listen, take some of our suggested actions, and in fact become happier. So, sometimes it does work — at least so it seems... initially...from that perspective anyway.

However, even when that happens, there is often an inherent negative. Lurking beneath the surface, almost in a seed form, ready to germinate and sprout at any given moment in the future.

The other person may harbor the feeling inside that they have been forced, cajoled, or at least artfully persuaded. And if that's the case, there may be a "bad taste in their mouth," feeling like their proverbial "Free Will toes have been stepped on" — that you did not give them a choice, or that you took their choice away from them. You "talked them into something" they really didn't want to do. (Parents: ever heard this from your kids? Kids: ever felt like saying this to your parents?)

"You *tricked me* into it!"

But, even if that's not the case, and they feel thankful, have we perhaps fooled ourselves in the short-term? *Fooled ourselves* into thinking that by helping other people experience happiness, we ensure *our own* happiness?

Said another way, does our happiness need to be dependent only on the results of our actions on others? Does our happiness need to be dependent on whether or not we are "successful" in helping other people be happy?

Now, keep in mind, when I say "happy" I'm using that in the most general sense of the word — so that could mean "be successful in their business," "successful in their relationships," "successful in (whatever pursuit in their life they are focused on)."

Instead, I think our happiness is and can be more internally driven, more "self driven."

What do I mean by that?

I think we can choose to derive our happiness more from *how* we interact, behave and communicate with others, rather than on the *result* of whether or not they follow our advice, and listen to us.

So, it's a *process* focus, rather than a *result* focus.

This does not mean that we don't focus on results. Results are very important, and do need to be focused on to accomplish actions effectively.

But remember, we're talking about *happiness* here. And placing our happiness in the "hands of others" and on whether they choose to make life choices that make us happy is risky at best and unpredictable for sure.

Now, I am a realist, and I am fully aware that the world we live in is a "Win-Lose" world. Our culture focuses — sometimes excessively — on winning and losing as the measure of happiness. This is of course flawed, but it is the reality of the culture we live in. And we are affected by it.

Look at the National Football League — it's the #1 sport in

the United States, an $11 billion business in which another $95 billion a year exchanges hands through gambling. This is not a sport that could survive based on looking at process only...it is Win-Lose, result-oriented.

However, the NFL does not represent the "game of life."

And those who have viewed the game of life as only a win-lose proposition, as a "results only" proposition, have left trails of broken relationships in their wake. Because that is not how life operates.

Life is relationships. A series of many relationships of many different colorations, types and qualities. And how we navigate those relationships determines our level of happiness in life.

Perhaps we might be happier if we took a more *process-oriented* approach towards those relationships. *Helping others in and of itself* may be a source of happiness for us that is equal to — maybe even greater than — the happiness that we might derive from whether or not our friends follow our advice.

And — keep in mind — maybe our suggestions have affected them in ways that are not readily apparent, so the "results" are not readily visible yet. Maybe we have had a positive impact on their lives and yet those helpful seeds still need some time to germinate.

Maybe this is another way to measure our success, another source of happiness for us. Being patient while the process plays out. And perhaps observing and enjoying the process as it unfolds.

Food for thought.

Give it a try, and let me know how it works for you.

Suffering & Happiness

Although I was Buddhist in several former lifetimes, I no longer view this world in terms of suffering. To me, this world is and can be full of enjoyment on many levels — mental, emotional and yes, physical.

Most Buddhists would not agree with that. They view this world as just a "way station" along their path to get to their "real world" afterwards, Nirvana.

Thus their views on suffering and "taking on the suffering of others" while here on Earth abound. Because this world is merely illusory to them, and of lesser importance.

I do not agree with that.

Moreover, others' suffering does not affect my ability to be happy. My deep empathy and sympathy for my clients' suffering does not "touch" or color my personal happiness. If it did, I could never do the intense healing work I now do with so many clients who are suffering and in so much pain.

Instead, I view my mind as a sovereign entity, as are all our minds. So when I help others who may be suffering, I can feel their pain without taking on their pain.

Their pain is not my pain. Their thoughts and emotions are not mine. That's the crucial distinction. That's what I mean when I say we are each "sovereign" — unique and distinct from each other — connected and communally related, but separate.

And so my happiness is independent of theirs.

To me, that's an extension of how and what Jesus taught us about "love." When we "accept others for who they are," we do not become them or take on their suffering. Yet we can be fully empathetic with them. That is truly loving them — and being able to help them most effectively from our independent state of happiness.

In this model, we act from a platform of inner power. While we can be emotionally moved by their plight, we remain spiritually untouched by their pain, not weakened or drained by their pain. And therefore, we then act from a position of strength to be able to help them overcome their suffering.

Again, this experience is automatic, spontaneous, inwardly driven, not contrived — that the suffering is theirs, not ours.

I resonate with Jesus's view rather than Buddha's.

I hope that perspective helps you in your personal pursuit of happiness as you make your own choices about how best to proceed in your life journey.

Can You Sprint Your Way To Happiness?

Note: I am the happiness guy.
But I'm the reality guy first.
Otherwise the feeling of happiness is just another
"fleeting feeling."
Here today, gone tomorrow.

Most Americans are sprinters. They sprint with their health, their finances and their relationships.

We treat our bodies like we're in an NFL game or on the battlefield.

People even say, "I'm on the battlefield of life..." Life is seen as a fight that must be "won."

Really?

We triage our bodies from one illness to the next. We "burn the candle at both ends." Over and over again.

And the pharmaceutical and insurance companies oblige enthusiastically. For them, the gift to their financial bottom line doesn't just come once a year — it's every day, 365 per year. And we each are complicit in contributing to their corporate power, market dominance and continued growth of their stockholder value.

We are addicted to them.

Quick. "Give me a shot of steroids so I can get back in the game, Coach!" And then within 10-20 years of retirement from the sport of life, the body gives out. And collapses. Crippled. Living on pain pills. Thinking that such a life is "normal" aging at age 40 or 50.

Yes, "normal" because the medical profession has arbitrarily deemed that unhealthy state "normal" for most — still living — human beings.

We've allowed ourselves to be fooled. It's *not* normal "healthy" aging to be on a dozen prescription medications.

It's...

Justification.

Call a spade a spade.

We knew better. But the immediate gratification was worth it! Wasn't it?

Most Americans do not have $400 in savings to pay for an unexpected expense. Studies tell us. Who's fault is that?

We can blame "the system." But that only goes so far.

Did you really need that second (third, fourth) flatscreen TV? Best Buy and Amazon love that you think you did!

But no worries. You can just file (yet another) bankruptcy and start the credit card game all over again. After all, you're patriotic. Right? Absolutely! Your consumerism is helping the American GDP, that's primarily based on our consuming *more and more* every year. Whether we need the stuff or not.

And what about our love lives?

Sad story. Sprinters. Not marathon runners. Short-term commitments. Lacking discrimination or discernment. Little focus. Intermittent at best. What, you say? I can't even write a full sentence here? (Chuckling, it's true.) I'm sprinting...sorry.

Ask yourself.

Are you a sprinter running as fast as you can from one crisis to another? From one relationship or dating app to another? Or are you a marathon runner in the game of life, enjoying it for the long haul?

Why?

Why are we Americans so enamored with the "short-term fix"? The quick jolt of bliss. Versus long-term contentment.

I think we have largely forgotten who we are.

We are not consumers.

We are not even Americans.

We are *minds with desires.*

And we would serve our own happiness more effectively if we looked more closely at *why* we have those desires. What drives them? And what therefore *drives us*?

Why do we feel the need to not take time for ourselves? And instead, get the "steroid shot" or pop the pain pill so we can get right back in the "rat race," back on the "hamster wheel" where we end up wearing ourselves out even more?

Why not cancel the relatives coming over and cooking for them...especially when you don't really like being with them and they don't appreciate you and your holiday hospitality anyway?

"Just because you do it every Christmas?" Is that a good enough reason?

Or… "But they'll be upset…" Oh! So *their* happiness is more important than *yours*? Hmmm… Could that perhaps be *why* you're so miserable? Self-devaluation?

Food for thought.

Take care of yourself. If you don't, who else will? Find help from friends, real friends...and if necessary, compassionate insightful professionals.

And keep the "long game" in mind.

If you sprint your way through life, you may burn out sooner than you like.

Sure. Maybe with more "stuff" (TVs, cars, clothes).

But with less happiness, more debt, and sadly perhaps, alone. Even if you're married.

Cotton Candy & Uncertainty

My roommate in college had this expression:

"It's all cotton candy...."

He would use it whenever someone was making an argument or talking about something in a way that made it sound better than it really was. What he was saying was that it was all sweetness with no substance.

Think about it. Makes sense, right?

Remember in your childhood when you went to that circus or county fair and your parents bought you a huge fluffy cotton candy on a cardboard tube? It was huge, right? Maybe 2 feet high, a foot wide! More than half your height at the time!!

But in a short few minutes it was in your tummy — all that sweet sugar — and that huge pink ball of "cotton candy" had literally disappeared into thin air. Because that's what it was mostly...*lots of air*. And enough sugar to make you feel good and excited!

I think that's what most of us are doing when we create institutions and belief systems that are not very well thought out. They are mainly there to make us *feel good*. Mostly they are lots of hot air and sweet comforting words.

We do it with religion, politics, and even in our general everyday conversations.

Cotton candy.

Why do we do that?

I think it's because of our perceived need for certainty in a universe that — confirmed from a physics standpoint — is fundamentally full of *uncertainty*. So, we need to be comforted.

But is that "cotton candy" approach to life realistic? Even helpful? Or does it actually lead to more pain and suffering?

I think the latter.

Because we can't fool our common sense mind, we can't ignore reality. The reality is that uncertainty is part of life.

And would we want it any other way? Would we want everything to be predictable? Wouldn't we get bored really fast?

But what happens when there's a disconnect? When there's a disconnect between our beliefs — which are often promulgated by our cultural, political, religious and spiritual institutions — and our experience of reality and thus our common sense?

We suffer.

First we get frustrated, and if we continue to ignore reality, we get angry and then despondent.

We have a "sugar crash" after we eat our societally-spun "cotton candy."

So what's the alternative?

Don't buy so much cotton candy. Don't eat all that sugar.

Eat healthier — in other words, *think for yourself*. Use your common sense. Match it against *your reality*.

Ask yourself — "Does it make sense?" If not, find a teacher, mentor or guide who gives you the insights and skills to help you think more clearly *for yourself*. Because when we figure things out for ourselves — even temporarily — it makes us feel more self-confident, more self-sufficient. More independent. More powerful.

And what does that, in turn, do? It makes us feel less concerned with — less bothered by — uncertainty.

Why?

Because we have then become so secure within ourselves by clarifying our thinking and cutting out all the stuff (the "hot air") that just fills empty space and doesn't make sense (all the "cognitive dissonance") that we feel like whatever may happen — whatever surprises we may encounter in life (or death) — *we'll be able to handle it.*

Maybe, even enjoy it.

Unconditional Love

What does it mean for it to be unconditional?
Does "unconditional" love make sense?
As compared to what?

L et's think about this phrase that we often hear —
"Unconditional Love."

PARENTAL LOVE

As a parent myself, I understand when parents often use this phrase to describe how they feel about their children. They mean, "It doesn't matter how badly my kids behave, whatever crazy stuff they do, I will feel deep affection for them and I will hold them close to my heart unconditionally — regardless, and forever."

I get that. That's what parents really mean when they say, "We love our kids unconditionally."

But, when it comes to relationships with lovers, partners, and others besides our kids, do we really mean that in the same way?

AS COMPARED TO WHAT?

Let's look at this through another lens, what I sometimes call my "As Compared to What?" lens —

What does unconditional love mean...*as compared to what*?

AS COMPARED TO CONDITIONAL LOVE

Can love be "conditional"?

I think that's the key point. Without even realizing it, subconsciously, people make it into being "conditional."

Conditional love looks something like this: "I will love you as long as you do this, or don't do this... as long as you are this way, or that way..." Sometimes it is spoken, but more often than not it is unspoken. Sometimes if the person is self-aware, they will know they are thinking it. But more often than not, we think and feel it subconsciously, without even knowing it is there.

Essentially what we are really saying is: "I will love you as long as you match *my ideal image* of...(a lover, husband, wife, friend, etc. — fill in the blank)."

And then, if the other person is aware of your desire, maybe he *forces himself* to change, and perhaps he (or she) does change to fit your image — *temporarily*. Then he goes back to who he really is...

Because that is inevitable.

Also inevitable is that he will feel *resentment* from forcing himself to change, even if it's supposedly "for a good reason." And if that resentment is allowed to continue and fester, it then turns into frustration and anger.

Not a good recipe for any relationship.

I think we all have experienced this to some degree at some point in our lives. But, if that anger is allowed to build up over time, to the point where the resentment becomes almost palpable, then the relationship is doomed — *divorce or separation is inevitable.*

Thus is the fate of *conditional love.*

Here's the thing...

We cannot deny who we really are — how we are wired through years, even lifetimes perhaps, of experience and practice. If any change is to occur, it must come *from inside ourselves*, it must be a decision we make unencumbered by the feeling that we are "doing it for the other person." We must "do it for ourselves."

By choice.

And, while having a vision — a mental idea — an ideal image — of what you may be striving for may be helpful, it can also be risky if you don't realize that you may be holding out for perfection in your life where it does not exist. Or worse — where you may be demanding perfection from, or possession of, someone or something outside of yourself *in order to be happy.*

Because just like love,

Our happiness should not be dependent on perfection,
or on anything outside of ourselves.

PERFECTION IN LOVE

Perfection is a lofty goal, but it is not reality.

In my other essays, I discuss the idea of perfection in greater detail and how it theoretically results in the reality of a static state — a state of no change, which we all know does not exist. We experience change in life all the time, not a static unchanging life. So, perfection is not real. It is aspirational at best, and I even question its value as aspirational.

LOVE IS ALREADY UNCONDITIONAL

So I think, either out of confusion, or maybe unsuccessful attempts at salvaging love in their lives, or quite frankly because perhaps they've been burned by lovers who had told them that they "love" them — people have created this term "unconditional" love.

But does the phrase even make sense?...

It's like saying "very unique" or the "most biggest"…isn't it? Unique and biggest are already "the most." Unique means "one of a kind." Not two or three of a kind! And you cannot get any bigger than the biggest. There is no such thing as "biggest plus one"!

Love is *already* unconditional. Otherwise it is NOT love. It is "liking" maybe, but it is *not* love. So, if you want to say "unconditional liking," that would be okay.

But...

Love is love. End of story. It's either a love story or not. It's not an "unconditional love" love story.

And this distinction is important, I think, because using unconditional implies the opposite exists, which, as we discussed, is the heart of the problem in the way most people love others — namely, conditionally.

But, I don't think "it's" that complicated.

"Love," that is.

LOVE IS NOT COMPLICATED

Love is not that complicated — at least not in theory. Most discussions about love do not start at the beginning, at the source...they tend to start somewhere down the road, well into the process of loving, liking, or appreciating others. But I think if we are to be at all successful in giving and receiving love, we must start at the source...ourselves.

And we must start *within* ourselves in a *different* way from what is typically discussed in most circles.

LOVE STARTS WITH SELF-ACCEPTANCE, TRUE SELF-LOVE

I think it starts with self-acceptance.

That may sound easy, but granted — *in practice* maybe it's not so easy for most of us mere humans! But that's the formula — at least *the formula* is simple...

Start with oneself, "turn within" — get to "know oneself" better, develop more self-confidence, *accept our flaws* and our strengths unconditionally. That is the tough part — accepting our flaws. This is true self-love.

Not merely the "Oh, I feel really good about myself right now because I just exercised" (or lost 5 pounds, or got a better job, a new client, or had a new baby...) type of self-love. That is not true self-love...that is merely *opportunistic* self-love.

Because true self-love is not bound by time and circumstance.

True self-love happens when we really know ourselves, our personalities, and most importantly when we embrace our "warts" — our weaknesses — all the stuff we may not like about ourselves.

And where does the ability and inner strength come from to be able to not engage in overly self-critical thinking, to love oneself *un*conditionally? It comes from starting on our inside first — by turning within, and relaxing our mind, body, emotions, and expanding our self-knowledge.

Thinking about our own personality — with all its quirks, oddities and imperfections — as beautiful. That is the basis for our being able to look at and appreciate fully — thus, "love" — that other personality we may be in a relationship with. That other person we may be "in love with."

THE WORLD

And by taking this more understanding, accepting, and clearer approach toward ourselves and how we view love *from within ourselves*, we will be more prepared to be loving human beings towards other people — towards our lovers, partners, and friends — towards all of the world *outside of ourselves*.

We will be more prepared to love — and yes, accept with all its warts and imperfections — our community.

The world community that we are a part of.

Love Is Not A Feeling

Most people think "love" is simply an emotion. An amorphous feeling inside. That's what most people are taught.

Most people teach that love is "feeling good," or "expressing good feelings" about others. A feeling that comes and goes. Something very indistinct that is "hard to nail down" but you know it when you feel it. It could also be defined as "the emotion caused by the attraction to something beautiful."

However, I want to suggest a different perspective on this popular concept.

I'm not suggesting that the above definition of love is incorrect. But I think it is limited.

Incomplete.

And that incompleteness I think can lead to disempowering the potential effects of this powerful idea. And worse, arguably sometimes creates suffering in our lives...in the name of "love."

I choose to define love in the way one of my early teachers taught us to love. Jesus said,

"Love is accepting the other person for who they are.
Not who you wish they were."

In his definition, love is not simply a feeling. Not a fleeting emotional response. It is definitely not merely a "feel good" feeling. And, it is not conditional.

It is an act. An act that can become a state of being.

What was he teaching us?

He was saying that, sure, we may all have expectations about what we desire in another person. How we hope they would interact and behave with us. How they might treat us.

But that is not ultimately up to us. It is up to them. It is molded and shaped by who they are, what their personality is, combined with choices they make in how they interact with each of us.

We do not control that. They do.

And our acceptance of who they are frees them up to be themselves with us in a way that makes them feel welcomed by us. Not judged by us.

And that increases the likelihood (nothing is ever guaranteed) that they may make choices in dealing with us that are in alignment with our needs, wants and desires at that moment.

That is — provided their intentions are similar to ours. And if we each desire a mutually beneficial outcome. Where we both can be happy and fulfilled.

But what if their expression — how they behave towards us — is not in alignment with what we want or need? What if it is hurtful? This is where most people's understanding of "love" falls apart. This is the crucial missing (or forgotten) component of that ancient teaching.

We walk away.

That was and still is the advice. It was his advice then, and it is my advice now. He never said, "Turn the other cheek."

He said we should see the other person "for who they are, not who we wish they were...." He said to recognize the snake for what it is, and treat it accordingly. So if what we see is harmful to us mentally, emotionally, or physically, we need to separate from them. Walk away.

And that is not only acknowledging who *they* are (in that 2,000-year-old definition of "love"), but it is also expressing our love for ourselves — "self love."

That is love and the expression of love the way I was taught to frame it many years ago. I have sometimes been successful in the application of that approach to love. And other times not so much.

None of us is perfect. So we need to be not so self-critical, not so harsh in our self-assessments. But we do need to aspire and attempt to move in the direction of this type of love: "*as acceptance.*"

That is…

If we want to truly pursue a sustainable level of contentment and happiness in our lives.

So today, as best I can, I continue to aspire to live that degree of love that I witnessed on a daily basis — for those three years 2,000 years ago.

Crying Is Not Weakness

We do a terrible job allowing ourselves to express emotions in our cultures worldwide. This problem does not just exist in the United States. I have clients now in 44 countries, and I've seen this problem everywhere, and in all social and economic strata.

When I say "emotions," I don't mean anger, because that emotion gets expressed quite freely in the world. And I think that particular emotion is a result of two things: not accepting reality the way it is, and pent up emotional frustration.

As a result, the most widespread and unfortunately, the most accepted emotion that we see on a daily basis is anger. We see it in many forms — mothers screaming at disobeying children, husbands abusing their wives, teenagers bullying their peers, and wars on many continents.

To be clear, I'm not here to address the complexities of all those different conflicts.

But I do want to address one aspect of expressing our emotions. Crying.

We can cry for many reasons...

Sadness or Happiness
Release of pressure
Longing for someone, something or someplace, or
Recognition — perhaps of an old relationship

But it's not a sign of weakness.

In fact, I think it's a sign of strength. It's a sign of inner strength. A sign that the person has a high enough sense of self-esteem that he or she doesn't care what others think and simply can express his/her emotions as they come up.

Remember what I just said when you see someone tearing up and apologizing for "being emotional."

Instead say, "No, it's ok for you to express how you're feeling in that way."

Acknowledge who they are at that moment in that simple way. By saying that, you are saying, as our Native American friends would say, that you "see" them.

Recognize that person as a strong person. Someone who may be more in touch with his inner self than you realize. An independent free thinking and feeling being.

Friendship

Jesus was a great teacher. But not in the usual ways people think of him.

His major influence on those who were close to him was his ability to demonstrate how to be a great teacher — without telling people what to do.

He taught by his example and by his friendship.

Those may sound like simple things, but I always say, "*in simplicity is profundity.*"

Teaching by example means that you have to "walk your talk" — and you need to walk it *consistently* so that the students see it in action all the time. That way they see it *frequently and repeatedly* which helps to inculcate in them the implicit and explicit lessons that are being taught.

And friendship is critical, because the basis of every relationship no matter how it is formally defined externally (marriage, dating, work colleague, teammate, friends or family) is the *internal friendship* between and among the people involved.

That means, as he taught us, we need to accept the other person — *however they present themselves to us.* In other words, to accept everything about them however they express it because that is "who they are."

That is true friendship.

All too often, we tend to be selective friends with others. Meaning that we tend to "pick and choose" what we like about them and what we will accept about them. Some of us even do it verbally, but most people do it at least nonverbally.

However, the other person feels that on some level — they sense it and know it even without your telling them. And that feeling of *non*acceptance, *not* fully accepting who they are, causes them to contract, to "feel smaller" so to speak, to *not feel loved*.

Jesus was a master at many things. But primarily I think he was a master at knowing people. Because he knew himself so well. By knowing himself so well, his mind was free to connect fully with other minds with whom he came in contact.

And they felt that deeply.

By connecting with them in that very personal way — even nonverbally — he was able to know things about them that may have been unseen, and certainly were often unspoken.

That is a different form of friendship.

It is a type of friendship that we can all have with anyone, whether we have ever met them before or not.

It is what I have aspired to my whole life — connecting with friends — as well as strangers — in a way that is deep and meaningful. No matter for how long. Whether it's a cab driver, a shoe repair guy, or a lawyer at a business reception — it doesn't matter. By simply accepting them for who they are at that moment, they open up, they relax — and they share a part of themselves with you — connecting even for a brief moment, as friends.

This, I think, is the most valuable lesson that he taught us.

Relationships Over Time

Have you ever had the experience with a close friend where you haven't seen them in a long time — maybe even many years — and yet when you get together with them, it's as if "*no time has passed*"? You pick up the conversation right where you left off the last time you saw them.

That is a clear indication of a very deep, and very old relationship. I think those types of relationships may go back even beyond this lifetime, and may be hundreds — maybe even thousands — of years old.

I have had many experiences like that in this lifetime with close friends. I have also had many experiences where I have had memories of having been with some of my friends and family of this lifetime in other lifetimes.

These sorts of stories are not uncommon in our culture, but most of the time we hear of the pleasant — the friendships — and not the other, not-so-pleasant types of relationships.

But, those exist as well, of course.

We've all had difficult relationships over time with family members, colleagues and even acquaintances. In other words, there are of course all manner of degree of relationships. Some closer, some more distant. Some more positive, some more negative.

That is reality. That is real life.

So let's talk a little bit about how to handle the *difficult* relationships we might encounter — again, in this lifetime. Because the easy ones are the close friendships, and we all know innately how to nurture those relationships. It's the difficult ones — the ones where we may even have been enemies in the past

— and now we are family members or work colleagues in this lifetime. Those are the difficult ones to manage.

What if the difficult relationship you're having now is with your father or mother or child...or your boss at work? What if you have some insight that that relationship goes beyond this lifetime, that it is very, very old?

First of all, I don't think the fact that we may remember having been with them before changes anything in terms of the "how" we manage the relationship in the "now." As I've emphasized in other essays, "living in the present" is paramount, regardless of whether we remember experiences from other lifetimes or not.

But if we do remember past experiences like that, then I suggest that we use them in a practical way. What I mean by that is to use the details we may recall from that memory of the past relationship to inform us both about ourselves and about the other person's personality and how he or she might behave with us now. Keep in mind that "nothing is written in stone," so we should use the data that we have and see if it's still appropriate now.

Keep it practical, and test it out in your relationship in the present. And keep in mind that people can change over time, albeit incrementally and typically slowly over very long periods of time. So, especially if it has been a very long time since you last interacted with that other person, he or she may have changed somewhat since your last encounter. Consequently, I suggest always giving the other person the benefit of the doubt.

That said, don't be stupid. What I mean by that is pay attention to the data that you do remember and apply it in that relationship accordingly. As I said, if it works, then that tells you that their personality probably has not changed that much since your last encounter.

So, whether they were even your enemies in another lifetime, it doesn't matter to this lifetime. This is the one that you're in now. And if that informs you somewhat in terms of your current relationship with them, that's fine. But remember, you're in the "here and now" with them.

Also keep in mind that life is about friendships and relationships — and managing all of them. That's the body of experience that we carry with us throughout the many lifetimes.

So, even if you remember that you were enemies in another lifetime, don't hold it against them.

We give ourselves opportunities in life to nurture, repair, expand, and at the very least revisit some of the relationships we've had. We should use these opportunities wisely. Not squander them.

That said, it's all about the choices we make. It's up to each of us to decide "if, how and when." There's no Master Plan — there's no one telling us what we should do.

It's up to each of us.

The Nuances Of Forgiveness

We've all heard of the concept of forgiveness. Or maybe we ourselves have even uttered the words,

"I forgive you…"

And many spiritual and religious circles encourage forgiving others, often stating outright that it is the "holy" or "righteous" or "giving" or "loving" thing to do. It is often made into a somewhat simplistic, almost trite act that "all good people should do."

They use the idea of forgiveness as if it implies, "I'm ok with the bad stuff you said or did. I'm not angry at you. And I don't hold a grudge against you for it."

And then, poof, everything is hunky-dory after that! Everything is fine.

I think it is more complicated and nuanced than that.

FORGIVENESS & LOVE

First, let's define love. Because I think love plays an intimate role in thinking about forgiveness.

"Love" — in the way I remember Jesus defined and exemplified it in his daily life — is "accepting the other person for who they are, not who you wish they were."

So let's keep that definition of love in mind as we think about the idea of Forgiveness. Not the Hollywood romanticized definition of love (as some feeling of butterflies in your tummy... which always goes away eventually after the initial newness of the infatuation wears off).

By using this definition of love as acceptance, we can

move away from "judging" the other person internally — their motives, their state of mind, their degree of self-awareness, etc. All of which are impossible to accurately discern and determine.

And instead, we can focus on the other person's *external* behavior. What they did or said. And how it affected us.

Forgiveness I'm defining as our decision to move on after accepting whatever that behavior by the other person was. We can either choose to move on *with* the other person or *without* them. But forgiving means we are moving on — mentally and emotionally — and yes, maybe physically.

Not forgetting what they said or did. Because no one ever forgets.

But moving forward. That is how I'm using the idea of forgiveness here.

DEGREES OF FORGIVENESS

FORGIVENESS AS A SIMPLE ACCEPTANCE OF "I'M SORRY"

Perhaps the simplest form of forgiveness is the one where the other person just slips up in a relatively minor way, maybe even unintentionally — what we used to call when I was a kid an "Oops" or a "boo-boo"...or maybe even a combination as in, "Oops, I made a boo-boo! Sorry about that!"

So then you say simply, "Yeah, no big deal. I forgive ya." And you both quickly move on.

That's the easy situation. The least intense. The almost non-thinking dispensing of forgiveness because whatever the other person perceived as "bad" behavior wasn't even that bad in your mind, or maybe was hardly even noticeable by you.

Love in the way we defined it is easy to implement. It's easy to accept the other person and what they did because it hardly had an impact on us. The forgiveness is more of an acknowledgement of their saying "I'm sorry" than anything else. Our "judgment meter" was barely turned on. The misstep in their behavior was hardly a ripple in the vast goodness of the ocean of our existing relationship.

We forgave them and moved on.

FORGIVENESS AS "I ACCEPT WHAT YOU DID AS AN EXPRESSION OF WHO YOU WERE AT THAT MOMENT, IT WAS BAD, AND I'M OK WITH IT"

A slightly more intense level of assessment on our radar gets triggered here.

Whatever they did — maybe they got in our face and criticized us for something they already knew we know we needed to act on. It's as if we say, "Okay, we've been down this road before, your behavior ticks me off, but I've chosen to live with it."

Why? Because we've chosen to love the other person in that way we described (accepting them for who they are, not who we wish they were). And their "bad" behavior is relatively minor and acceptable, as far as our relationship is concerned.

It's a bit more intense than the first situation because we are ill-affected by the behavior and it does bother us, but again, it is more than a slight ripple, maybe like a wave but still relatively minor on the vast ocean of that relationship.

FORGIVENESS AS "I ACCEPT WHAT YOU DID AS AN EXPRESSION OF WHO YOU WERE AT THAT MOMENT AND I'M *NOT* OK WITH IT"

In this situation, we need to assess both their behavior and how it affects us more deeply. First, as always, we are assessing the other person's behavior as acceptable or not.

And where that line is varies from person to person. We are not a monolithic human race who all act and react the same to all situations. We are each unique.

Forgiveness is not a blind act. It may be in theory. But it

never is in reality.

And the last time I checked, we live in reality. Not in some world of theory.

So, when I forgive you for whatever you did that I assessed as bad (maybe hurtful, or inappropriate in some way), I have a choice. I can choose to stay in the relationship or not.

The reality I need to accept is that if I stay in the relationship, I am continuing to accept the potentiality of more of that same bad behavior. Because as the saying goes, "the leopard does not change his spots."

In other words, people don't change overnight. Behavior does not change overnight. It takes a long long time, many years, arguably many lifetimes to change deep-seated personality traits that are the source of our behavior, good and bad.

So by making the choice to stay in the relationship, we are choosing to accept the behavior. Make no mistake about it — we need to be clear in our own minds that we are in fact *making that choice*. By our very action to stay. Even if we say, "I forgive you."

Said another way, we should not delude ourselves into thinking that since we had a conversation with the other person about the bad behavior, and since we forgave them, that that mere conversation and dispensing of forgiveness will change their behavior. The change in their behavior has to come from within themselves, not from our persuading them to change. Nor by our forgiveness.

Forgiveness frees *us* up — it does not necessarily change *them*.

FORGIVENESS AS "I ACCEPT WHAT YOU DID AS AN EXPRESSION OF WHO YOU WERE AT THAT MOMENT, I'M DEFINITELY NOT OK WITH IT, AND SEE YOU LATER"

In this most intense situation, we have decided that enough

is enough. And notwithstanding however many conversations we have had with the other person, we have decided that the level of their bad behavior is such that it is no longer mutually beneficial for us to stay together.

Nevertheless, we can still end the relationship with forgiveness in the way I have suggested here. By moving onward, and going our separate ways. And without anger — because we have accepted them for who they have been (we have not resisted that reality, otherwise that resistance to who they are would have caused us frustration and anger).

So then, even in this most extreme intense situation, we can still move on with forgiveness and love (as acceptance) for the other person. We can choose to do so because the relationship is no longer mutually beneficial. We are no longer being nurtured by the other person in our relationship — at least not enough to make staying worthwhile.

Moving on in this way would perhaps be a way to demonstrate not only our respect and love for ourselves — the ultimate in self-love — but also showing our maturity as a soul living with and relating to other souls in our many and varied relationships throughout our lives. A demonstration to ourselves and to the world that nothing is perfect nor does anything last forever, so moving on may be the appropriate and healthy thing to do.

The Dangers Of Emotionally Feeling Good

I just watched a documentary on Netflix about a religious group whose members would do wild meditations jumping around in apparent ecstasy.

Now, don't get me wrong. Feeling good is generally a good thing. But is it *everything*? And is it the best metric to use to assess something's value in our life?

Merely judging our sense of happiness and well being against whether we *emotionally feel good* is the norm in our world culture. There is no doubt about that.

Just look at most best-selling self-help books, workshops and gurus, TV ads ("buy this and feel good"), the pharmaceutical and mental health industry ("take this pill and feel good"), religious teachers ("believe this whether it makes sense or not because it'll make you feel good"), and even our educational system ("read this version of history because it'll make you feel good about your country").

Basically any sector of our society. They all preach this "feel good" notion of happiness.

But is it accurate? Is it foolproof?

IT'S RISKY

What can make us feel good?

Many things can...

- High self esteem
- Good physical health
- Healthy diet
- Loving friends

- Meditation
- Exercise

All those are arguably good for us.

But what about...

- Alcohol?
- Drugs — prescribed and "recreational"?
- Groups that support our beliefs, whether religious, cultural or political — at the exclusion of others?
- Cults?

Hmmmm...maybe not so great for our short or long-term health. Alcohol is a neurotoxin, drugs have negative side effects, and exclusionary groups and cults limit our thinking to "their" thinking.

But...wait a minute, they make us *feel good*, don't they?

THE POWER OF EMOTION

It is indisputably powerful.

All emotions whether positive or negative are strong moving forces in our psycho-emotional daily life. Excitement. Joy. Serenity. Love. Anger. Sadness. Fear.

So it's no wonder that we all gravitate towards them. However, not only do we naturally experience those feelings — I mean you cannot prevent it — but — and here's the rub — we also have a tendency to place more weight, more credibility in them as metrics, i.e., as a yardstick, to measure many of the choices we make in life.

Why?

Because the "feeling of feeling" is so intoxicating. So alluring. Even if it's not just feeling good. Even the feeling of feeling badly can be intoxicating to some. Or the feeling of feeling fear — just look at how popular death-defying rides at amusement parks are...

And when the feeling is so intoxicating, we sometimes

shelve our thinking — yes, even our common sense — in the hope of continuing that enjoyable feeling. Sometimes even well past the point when we "knew better."

Ever experienced that in, let's say, a relationship? "I knew I should have left him months ago, but it was so thrilling to be with him…" Surely, you've heard both men and women say that refrain.

THE POWER OF THINKING

I know that some people put thinking and feeling in the same category. After all, they're both mental experiences, right?

But at least for the purposes of our discussion here, I think it's helpful to separate them and look at them individually.

"Thinking" I'm defining for our narrow purposes here as "thinking rationally, analytically, clearly without cognitive dissonance."

I think we all understand what thinking rationally and analytically means. In layman's language I think we would call it "using our common sense."

What I mean by "thinking clearly without cognitive dissonance" is not coming to conclusions or making statements that do not make logical sense with our thinking process or prior statements. In other words, coming to conclusions that just don't fit with what we are saying. Without cognitive dissonance means thinking free from stuff that doesn't make sense, or said another way, it's without contradictions, it has logical consistency.

For example, telling our kids: "Stop playing video games for hours on end! You should give your brain a rest and go outside and get some exercise!" — while we sit on our couch day and night watching hours of TV. That's cognitively dissonant. In layman's language we sometimes call it "sending a mixed message," or "setting a bad example." We should more honestly call it "a wrong message."

Or, the health coach or healthcare professional who treats patients and advises them to exercise regularly, and make healthy food choices — yet himself eats at fast food drive-through windows and smokes cigarettes.

And of course all of these examples affect us individually, personally, when we are the "dissonant actor." We are not immune to the ill effects of thinking and acting dissonantly. It can cause inner confusion, relationship problems, and can even negatively affect our physical health.

So we can all probably agree that thinking clearly is important. Not only for good parenting, but also for our own individual health and well being.

The problem is that for most people "thinking clearly" is a big, giant snooze. It's boring. It just ain't sexy!

It does not "juice us." Where's the tingle, the chills, the shudder?

Right?

I know. I know.

AN EMOTIONAL NEED

But…

What if *thinking clearly* became an "emotional need"?

What if you somehow found a way to become "juiced," uplifted, even excited by thinking? And then even *more* excited by thinking *more* clearly about yourself, your life, your surroundings, the world, the universe…

That's what I've come to realize about myself. You could call it a self-realization. Something that I've learned about myself in my eternal quest in response to my inner voice — "Know Thyself."

It makes me happy to understand more fully and to be able to think more clearly about myself and life's issues. And even more so by sharing that to help others. I find that emotionally fulfilling. Okay, you may say I sound weird…and you wouldn't be the first to think that!

FINAL THOUGHTS — BUYER BEWARE

But here's the main thing to consider.

Please understand that I don't think emotions and emotional needs are — at all — inherently bad. But relying solely on "feeling good" as our yardstick in life can be risky and potentially dangerous. It can lead to blind action and blind following. That is, acting blindly by yourself, say in a toxic relationship. Or blindly following others without regard for one's own common sense. Without thinking clearly.

And their self-interests may not align with yours. They may even be totally opposite to yours without your knowing it.

But again, it's not *the feeling* that is bad. It's the blindness that can often result.

So *caveat emptor* ("buyer beware"). Or perhaps "thinker beware." Our thinking mind needs to beware of being overshadowed by its feeling side, at the risk of our real happiness.

Ignoring that balance can be dangerous to one's health
and well being.

Chapter 3

LIFE PRINCIPLES

Grieving The Loss Of Normalcy During The COVID-19 Pandemic

What is "normalcy"?

It's different for each person. For some it may mean going to work or school every day, dealing with the daily commute, for others it is taking the children to school and picking them up afterwards, for some it may be alone time away from one's spouse and children and now — during the COVID-19 pandemic — everyone is shut in (trapped) under the same roof and in each other's space!

Each of us has our own "normal" life that's been disrupted. When that disruption occurs, discomfort sets in.

And soon afterwards we start yearning for our normal life again. And then when that doesn't happen, often overwhelming sadness and conflicting feelings set in. Sadness that we miss our "normal" daily life, and conflicted because we know we have to be secluded for our own health and others, but we don't like it. Maybe we even feel guilty or selfish for feeling that way...we are conflicted inside.

Grief.

That's what we're experiencing then. Grief.

That's the scenario that has happened over the millennia during the time of every pandemic that humankind has known. Smallpox in Ancient Rome, bubonic plague in the Middle Ages, flu epidemics in the early 20th century, and now the COVID-19 pandemic. To name a few.

How do we best handle that Grief that often arises, so that it doesn't debilitate us?

First of all, we need to understand that a "loss" can be a loss of almost anything: our normal life routine, illness, death of a loved one, job layoff, divorce, no graduation ceremony with our classmates, retirement income loss, etc. And a pandemic like we are seeing now can cause any of those, and more.

Then, we need to ask ourselves — because the following is a *choice*:

"Do we want to recover from our grief and be more fully present in life going forward, or do we want to just distract ourselves from it temporarily?" Because the temporary fix is often the easy way out, but not the most effective...e.g., self-medicate with alcohol or drugs, binge watch Netflix, and the like.

But that's just a band-aid. After it wears off, you're still grieving. You still feel really sad, upset, and conflicted about how you're feeling.

Before we talk about what to do, let's talk briefly about what NOT to do.

Myths about Grief:
1. "Don't feel badly"
2. "Grieve alone"
3. "Be strong for others"
4. "Replace the loss"
5. "It just takes time"
6. "Just keep busy"

Those common myths do not work. In fact, when people give us that advice, it often frustrates or even angers us. Because, we *do* feel badly, so don't go telling me *not* to!

Another myth or misunderstanding:

Grief is not = to sadness

We don't lose the sadness when our loved one isn't here anymore. In fact, I think the depth of sadness is directly proportional to the depth of love we have for that person.

Finally, another partial understanding that can lead to unnecessary suffering:

Elisabeth Kübler-Ross did not mean for her study of terminally ill patients to become the absolute "5 Stages of Grief" for *all* losses...it was a non-scientific study (a survey of patients who were dying in a hospital). Groundbreaking for its time in the 1960's when few acknowledged grief, it was not, however, based on a large group of people experiencing many forms of loss. She later said she never meant them to be treated like pillars of stone — stages that everyone had to go through when grieving. But her seminal work was key to moving forward our understanding about grief.

So...

What is "Grief"?

Here's how I think of it:

1. *Overwhelming* sadness associated with a loss, and

2. *Conflicting* feelings caused by the change in a familiar pattern of behavior (mental, emotional or physical)

Key with #1 is reducing and eliminating the "overwhelming" part. We may never lose the sadness. For example, I'm still sad about my mom dying suddenly during my 3rd year of Boston College Law, but I no longer have the *overwhelming* feelings of sadness that used to sometimes paralyze me.

And I have recovered and resolved the *conflicting* feelings I had over the loss of my mother — e.g., she would say, "Don't waste your time coming to visit me at the (Norwood) Hospital! You need to study!!" So should I listen or should I go? Conflict. After she died, I was haunted by thoughts of: "Should I have ignored her and visited more? It's too late now!" Conflict. That conflict I've resolved. That grief I've thus recovered from.

What to do:

1. Acknowledge your sadness, confusion, fear about the loss or potential loss — do not "stuff" or bury your emotions — it's ok to be bummed out about your lack of normalcy, or no income and feeling insecure about the future. This is a worldwide pandemic and everyone is affected. You're not alone in how you feel.

2. Talk about your feelings openly with someone you trust, who has a non-judgmental "listening ear" — e.g., a close friend, family member, or therapist.

3. Be in the present moment. If the loss is "potential" and not actual — e.g., about maybe losing someone — spend time with them now, even virtually on the phone or video — on FaceTime or Facebook/Instagram videophone. Or if it's about "maybe" losing your job, remind yourself you have NOT been laid off and you are still collecting a paycheck.

4. Be honest with yourself and your feelings. I am not a proponent of ignoring reality. Yes, it's often helpful to look at what we have, not what we don't have. But when we are in pain, we need to acknowledge it, talk about it with others if we can. Not bottle it up and make believe everything is fine, when it's not. (Trust me, I've tried it and it does not work!)

5. The Uncertainty associated with this pandemic is normal. Natural. Everyone is experiencing it. Again, you're not alone.

6. Control what you can. And let go of trying to control what you can't.

7. Take action. If you've been laid off, look for a job that you can do from home, at least for now. If you're just

at home temporarily and still will have your job later, exercise in your house or go for a walk in the sunshine. Don't just sit and eat junk food.

8. Isolate yourself as we've been instructed, wash your hands, keep them away from your face, sleep more, drink more water. Watch less TV news. You have control of your TV remote! Wear a mask and social distance when you go out.

9. "Turn within" through meditation or other means to relax and rejuvenate to strengthen your immune system. This is important to manage and reduce your anxiety so it doesn't weaken your internal chemistry by triggering the "Fight or Flight" excessively.

10. Maintain perspective — during World War II we had 70,000,000 deaths worldwide. 3% of the world's population died in 6 years. Today that would be the equivalent of 228,000,000 people. And even back then — as terrible as those huge losses were — the world rebounded fairly quickly afterwards. We have a strong human spirit worldwide that we should recognize and remember.

Those are some beginning self-help steps we each can take.

And if you're still overwhelmed by the feelings of grief — the overwhelming sadness and anxiety about the unknown, and conflicting feelings about all of this — call me.

At the end of this pandemic — and yes, it will eventually end — my hope is that it will inspire us to be less tribal. Remind us that we're all human beings.

The virus doesn't care about our color, religion or beliefs. We all have similar fears, concerns, needs and desires. And in the end, making sure we all have enough food, shelter...and yes, hand sanitizer and toilet paper...is all in everybody's best self-interest.

Balance

"Lack of extremes."
"Balance is evenness."
"All or nothing."
"Balance is passivity."

These are some of the beliefs people have about balance.

"Balance is 'either/or.' Balance is boring. Balance is impossible. Seeking balance leads to frustration."

No.

This is a conflation of what balance is. And that misunderstanding is actually understandable — especially in our world.

We live in a world that is *externally* focused. It's all about "doing," about "results," about "what we can see and touch." It is a "materialistic" world. And I don't mean economically. I mean we're into "identifiable things, actions." These are the XYZ's of life that I refer to in some of my other essays.

But is that all there is? And is that how we should assess "balance" in our lives?

Is balance always about giving something up to replace something you find more important? Maybe *sometimes* it is — e.g., leaving a work project partially completed in order to rush off to catch your child's school musical.

But not always.

And I would maintain that the most important balance is completely missed by those who would argue that a balanced life is "boring."

True balance comes from the inside out. What do I mean by that?

I mean that we need to feel connected and anchored within ourselves, our minds need to be comfortable with who we are on the deepest levels of our minds for us to be truly self-confident, and inwardly strong. If we don't become truly connected within ourselves, everything we do to strengthen ourselves is just really window-dressing. It's not anchored. And therefore, it is easily shaken.

That is the source of balance in life. Being unshaken.

Because if we are anchored inside ourselves, by having regularly "turned within" and developed that comfortable, conscious connection with ourselves, then our outward life also becomes more dynamic, more creative, more expansive in its opportunities and liveliness. In other words, it is far from boring.

Ironically, I suspect that even those who may have incorrectly or incompletely measured balance only by looking at the XYZ's of life — i.e., how many actions they accomplished versus how many they had to give up in order to create the supposed balance — would agree that if one could do all of that external stuff and still maintain a sense of inner calm and inner strength at the same time, that would also be a way to define "balance" in life.

And the "action only" crowd is not the only group among us who misinterprets what balance means.

Many New Age spiritual followers also conflate and confuse this.

Seeking *less* activity in the world — spending years in ashrams, hours in daily meditation — is often based on an underlying belief that the physical world is less desirable than the "inner, spiritual" world. It is a form of denial of who they are. They define their "real self" as that inner part of themselves.

73

But that is just a *part of* their reality. They choose to deny the existence of the physical.

Unfortunately, this may sometimes have unexpected, unhealthy physical consequences for these spiritual seekers due to their extreme inactivity. At the very least, it has the consequence of minimizing the individual's life experience possibilities. By making that choice, by definition, the individual has chosen to not take advantage of the fact that he or she is in a physical body in this lifetime.

And while Free Will dictates that they can always make that choice, I question whether or not it promotes balance in life. Because it often leads to more passivity, less engagement in the world.

And ironically, that is also a "materialistic" view of balance. Because it also measures balance by levels of activity. It's also still focused on the XYZ's of life. Essentially, without realizing it, they are fully engaged in a form of "spiritual materialism."

So, what's the bottom line?

Balance does not mean running away from actions. Balance does not mean "lesser." It does not mean "taking away."

Balance means going inside and then coming out, and fully engaging head on, "full on" with the world. *In whatever way* you may choose to do so.

But, it should *never* come from a place of lacking.

Balance — true balance — comes from a place of *fuller* connection with oneself inside, so that one can *fully engage* with the world on the outside. And with that stronger inner connection, one then has the faculties to make choices in one's external life that promote more external balance – with oneself, with one's family and friends, and with one's community.

Ego

Note: I am not discussing "ego" in psychological terms here. I am looking at it through the spiritual filter.

What about this idea in some spiritual circles that "ego is bad"? Limiting. A negative part of, or description of us. I strongly disagree.

REDEFINITION

Ego, for me, means individuality. It is therefore neutral. Neither good nor bad. It is just a descriptive term.

How we express that individuality is up to each of us.

I think we tend to insert a negative, limiting connotation to "ego" when we sometimes — within ourselves — feel limited and helpless. We have all been there.

But our individuality is who we are. We are each unique, vibrant, sentient beings.

Individuals.

And there is a profound beauty in that reality. Accepting that is true "self-love." Not accepting that is self-loathing.

We often hear people use the term "unconditional love." As I have spoken about on other occasions, that is a redundant term. Love means "accepting the other for who they are, not who we wish they would be."

So, loving ourselves *already* means accepting who we are without conditions.

And we each are individuals. With uniquely operating minds (souls, spirits, consciousnesses — all synonymous) and we need to accept and embrace that fact if we are truly "walking our talk" about love and self-love.

Otherwise we are just talking and wasting our breath. Preaching but not acting. Spiritually fraudulent.

THE SHIFT

So what is the missing link? How do we make the shift to more fully accepting our individuality — our "ego" sense of self?

First step, make the recognition that we just discussed.

Next step, turning within.

By regularly practicing a technique of effortlessly "turning within," we automatically begin to nurture and strengthen the connection with ourselves, deep within. And by releasing our physical and emotional stresses, and expanding our conscious capacity for mental-psychic experience, we can begin to directly experience the profundity and vastness of who we truly are as human beings. We begin to break the self-imposed limitations. We no longer feel helpless. We feel confident, secure.

We can then experience the sublime power and expansive connectedness we each have within ourselves and can begin to express that outwardly to the world around us — our friends, loved ones, acquaintances and yes, strangers.

But this recognition and acceptance of our individuality — and thus ego — as a starting point, is key. Only from that initial understanding can we blossom and grow in our own self-love before we can share that with others — in our families, our work, our lives.

Negating our ego, our individuality, is a non-starter. Why start by shackling, by limiting ourselves?

Of course I understand it is usually neither conscious nor intentional. Understandably, it often comes from a place of vulnerability and helplessness.

But it can be turned around and our individuality made to

be a source of strength by "turning within" and experiencing the greatness that lies within us — that is an integral part of "who we are" as individual beings, as beings of light who are temporarily in the bodies of human beings.

From that place of inner power, self-confidence and self-knowing, we can truly begin to experience what life as an individual living on Earth can be.

Earth — A Planet Of False Hopes, Dreams & Expectations

We live on a planet inhabited by humans who are addicted to being inspired. But who have little interest in taking the actions required to fulfill those hopes, dreams and expectations that inspire them.

Why is that?

I wonder if it's because we are so enamored by those who are enthusiastic about (fill in the blank...religion, politics, education, finance, family, whatever) that we stop there at the sight of enthusiasm. And promptly follow whatever has initiated that enthusiasm.

Why? Because it feels good!

Right? It "feels good" to be enthusiastic. To be inspired.

But is it wise to stop there and just follow the enthusiastic throng?

I think not.

There are many examples throughout history where the enthusiastic throng was proven to be on the "wrong side of history" — the 1919 Treaty of Versailles that arguably led to the creation of Nazi Germany, 1930's Germany and its nationalistic fervor, religious oppression of the Holy Inquisition in the 1200's, Mao and his Cultural Revolution that killed 3 million and persecuted 100 million, and slavery worldwide for millennia as a means of maximizing business profit.

What they all have in common was that the masses — or enough of the masses in those regions — were enthusiastic in their support of whatever.

What was lacking was any forethought about what obvious — and especially the unseen, the unintended — consequences would likely result from those actions.

What was missing?

Rational thought.

The problem with rational thinking is that it's not "sexy." It doesn't give you an immediate thrill. It doesn't make you tingle like "enthusiasm" does — even if the enthusiasm is misplaced.

But I have found that thinking rationally — asking "does it make sense?" — has brought about more long lasting happiness for me than merely following the latest hope, dream or expectation driving the most recent enthusiastic reaction from the pedestrian on the street.

Sure, it's not as flashy and tingly. But my happiness — my long term happiness and inner contentment — is worth more to me than some fleeting "feel-good" experience based on some unfounded hope, dream or expectation created by someone or some group I don't even know.

And while we're on the subject of rationally assessing our decision making and sources of enthusiasm and inspiration, let's address some of our friends on the Other Side.

Angels — especially the ones who have charged themselves with looking after Earth's inhabitants — are doing no one but themselves a favor by promoting enthusiastic thinking about the false belief that the world will be enlightened overnight, that some "Renaissance" is coming to Earth "soon," perhaps following the next winter solstice, planetary alignment, solar eclipse, or presidential election....

First, this popular age-old spiritual myth violates the principle of Free Will.

No angel or "god" — or external planetary force — can

force someone to be loving and kind if they don't want to be.

And second, do the psychics, mediums and spiritual teachers channeling this message from their sources on the Other Side not read history? Do they not know that angels and others over "there" have been singing this same song for millennia?

And...uh-hem. Has the world in 2020 become that "enlightened" planet after all those thousands of years of similar "predictions"?

Do those claims even pass the "common sense" test?

I am here to inspire. But I choose to inspire through realism *and* idealism. Not merely through the latter alone.

Here is why.

Because my experience over the past several thousand years watching so many — who have been enthusiastic and inspired, only to later become dejected and depressed when they don't see the turnaround as quickly as their hopes, dreams and expectations had led them to believe — has taught me we need to take the "long view" on helping our fellowship of humankind to progress and develop.

Let's assume humans have been on Earth for 400,000 years, give or take a few years. We have definitely progressed and become less cruel. We no longer have entire cultures sacrificing women, children (and some men) to "satisfy the gods." But look how long it has taken for that limited but noticeable degree of progress to take hold in our cultures worldwide. And even then, there is still so much more to be done in reducing cruelty on our planet.

So can we and should we continue to work as helpers of our planet — on cruelty, climate change, inequality — yes, absolutely. But we need to take the long view and not be discouraged if the successes we hope for do not materialize as fast or in the manner we expect.

Transcending Cruelty — Getting Beyond Bullying

Note: None of what we discuss below is meant to absolve or give a "free pass" to the bully. On the contrary, the cruel person is and always will be responsible for their actions, and for the consequences created by them. However, this discussion is meant to shed some light on WHY the bully acts the way he or she does — so that we can better understand their motives, and thus hopefully find a way to counter their bad behavior. To neutralize their bad behavior as much as possible, without feeding it any further.

So, what about "mean" people, or bullying? Or, racial stereotypes, ethnic slurs, religious wars, ethnic cleansing, office politics, etc.? All those unpleasant types of behavior that, if directed at us or those we love, make us cringe, recoil in disgust, or maybe even cower if we indeed feel truly intimidated — what can we do about it?

There are two concepts I want to introduce to our discussion:

1. "Transcending Cruelty" and
2. "The Importance of Being Important"

These two *concepts* may be new in the framework of the discussion around cruelty and bullying, but bullying and cruelty of course are not new *experiences* to us — we encounter them unfortunately all too often. We may have been the recipients, the victims of bullying ourselves, or we may have watched others being bullied either on the public stage in the media, or perhaps closer to us in our family or work situations where we were a bystander. Or, maybe at moments in our lives, we have been the bully.

CRUELTY AND BULLYING

First, what is "cruelty"?

Cruelty is *"when someone enjoys inflicting pain or unhappiness on another."* So it could be physical or emotional pain. Or both.

And what's the motivator for doing this?

Ironically, the motivator is the same motivator that motivates any of us to do anything — the pursuit of happiness.

However, in this case the person inflicting the cruelty is so unhappy, so miserable within him (or herself) that to make himself happy, he must make those around him *more* unhappy than he is, at that moment.

Think about it. Think of all the bullies you've ever experienced or observed in your life. Up close or from afar. Are they truly happy people?

Don't be fooled by their boastful talk, their bravado, their chest beating about how strong they are, how magnanimous they are, how smart they are, how much money they have, how big their house is, how fancy their car is. That is the typical bully smokescreen. It's always about being "the best" and "the most." Even the humility is contrived — "I am the most humble person on Earth; no one is more humble than I am." But that sort of behavior is a HUGE red flag. Those are all the common signposts of a weak sense of self — in a word, insecurity. In another word, unhappiness — *deep inside.* Smiling on the outside, miserable on the inside. Thus the need to constantly prop themselves up by boasting and bragging.

Makes sense. Rings true, doesn't it? Sound familiar? We've all seen it — on the international and national stage, in our towns and cities, in our workplaces, and yes, even in some of our homes.

"THE IMPORTANCE OF BEING IMPORTANT"

So, what is the bully's solution? And why does the bully resort to depressing all of those around him or herself? What is the essence of why they mistreat others the way they do?

It's quite simple actually.

Making others around him/her feel more miserable than he/the bully feels, in turn, allows the bully to feel "more important" or more powerful than the person he is being cruel to. And that feeling makes the bully feel good. Really good. Really powerful.

Really important.

At least temporarily.

It is that feeling of being *more important* that then becomes central to that person. It becomes central to his or her ability to make him/herself happy. And so, it often becomes an obsession for the bully — a feeling that they essentially *live for*.

Thus, the concept of *"the importance of being important"* becomes their central life theme. Look closely, and you will see it play out over and over again throughout the bully's life. Depending on their degree of insecurity, in extreme cases it could even play out on a daily basis, even multiple times a day. Verbal and nonverbal messages of "I'm more important than you are, more important than he is, more important than she is..." Those are the red flags, the signposts of insecurity, the markings of a bully.

And I think it bears mentioning in this world of reality TV stars and celebrity obsession, that no matter how "en vogue" it may be to argue this following point in certain aristocratic circles of society, there is no truth to the fallacy that anyone is better in any way than anyone else merely "based on your breeding or your family genealogy."

Yes, someone may be more powerful than you politically, socially or economically. But never psychologically — and in the broadest, most non-religious way — never spiritually. We are each of us "spiritually and psychologically sovereign beings." We can always say "No" to the bully. In that sense, we can always choose individual freedom.

It doesn't matter how powerful the person seems on the surface. Regardless of where you fall in relation to the bully in the economic, social, political, or educational food chain — whether he's the president, prime minister, king, emperor, CEO, religious or spiritual leader, or the owner of the company or plantation, we each have the power as free-thinking individuals to agree or disagree with whatever he tells us. And if they bully us, by our understanding these dynamics, we each can stand more powerfully upright facing their inappropriate behavior and do whatever we need to do to retain our personal dignity and individual fortitude.

We will discuss specific actions we can take in further detail below.

I also think it is valuable to realize that, if forced to self-reflect, the bully typically would *not* define himself (or herself) as a cruel or mean person. If you asked him if he was cruel, he would say, "Of course not! Look at all the wonderful things I do for others!"

But in questioning him further you would find that he really enjoys being important. That is a red flag. A signpost to look deeper. Because it's that feeling of being more important than someone else that drives the bully, becoming a functional need — a "raison d'être" — that makes him feel good about himself.

That often defines who s/he is. Often how s/he himself proudly defines who s/he is, and if asked, s/he would answer: "Look at how important I am — I am more important than you are."

Most bullies are subtle about how they lord themselves

over others. However, the bold ones who state their importance to your face are the ones who have found that their bullying works time and time again — but through their "in your face" behavior, without realizing it, they are revealing their deep-seated insecurity to you. The more "in your face" they are, the more insecure they are. Pay attention and recognize that for what it is.

And remember, since the "feel good" effects of bullying are temporary, to continue that feeling of importance, the bully must continue to make people around him feel weaker, more miserable. And then as he craves even more happiness for himself, he tends to turn up the "misery intensity" dial and make that one group (or one person) more and more miserable, or maybe even widen the group adding more people to it, more people to taunt, belittle and name-call — otherwise he is no longer sufficiently "more important."

The more miserable he makes his victims, the more superior, important, and thus happy he becomes. It is a vicious cycle. But in the bully's small-minded "me-only" world of narcissism, it works.

THE ILLUSION

So, the odd thing here, you could even say "the illusion" here is that the person who is being cruel (the bully) continually has to surround himself with people who are *more miserable* than he is, people who feel weaker and at his mercy, and thus more unhappy than he is.

And, you might ask: "What kind of life is that?" Surrounding yourself with weak and unhappy people? People you *want* to be unhappier than you, whom you want to feel weak and powerless around you? People who are sycophants, ass-kissers just to keep you — the bully — happy?

But you see, since that person, the bully, is neither aware

of nor understanding his own behavior, he does not see that illusion. The bully only *feels better*, and because *their* feelings are all that matter in their mind — it is ALL about them — that is where they focus. That is *all* that matters in their little self-centered world...their small universe in which the only person who matters is them.

TRANSCENDING CRUELTY

So...what can be done about this?

Let's talk about the concept of "Transcending Cruelty."

This concept applies *both* to the person being cruel, and to the person who is being made miserable by the cruel person.

THE BULLY

First let's address the bully, who actually is the more difficult person to help.

If the cruel person realized the above illusion that we described, he or she would find that they might not derive as much happiness from their actions as they previously thought. I mean, really? — Surround yourself with weaker and more miserable people than you are...?! Seems like a world you or I would not want to live in, but as you might guess, the bully is not typically a very self-aware, self-reflective individual.

That's right, realizing that illusion, takes a more self-aware individual to first perceive and then accept that understanding, and by definition, the cruel person is most likely feeling miserable in the first place because of a low sense of self-esteem, a lack of self-confidence, which starts with a lack of self-awareness. So that is the proverbial Catch-22, and any significant level of positive change for that bully will probably take a much longer time than any of us has the patience for.

But, in a nutshell, the solution for the bully is to do some serious personal development work — meditation and personal therapy or other similarly deep mental-emotional work — and deal with his or her insecurities, strengthen themselves from within, and develop a stronger sense of self which would engender more self-confidence and less of a need to feel so "high and mighty" over others manifesting in forms of bullying and cruelty.

And for those of you who know me, I am an "idealistic pragmatist." So, the idealistic side of me demands that I lay that path out for the bully, but the realist side of me requires that I point out that the probability of a bully taking that self-aware route is minimal at best, depending of course on the degree of insecurity within the bully.

Now, let's turn to the second issue of how to help the person who is being treated cruelly, how to help them "transcend cruelty."

THE VICTIM

RECOGNITION

The first step to helping the victim deal with the bullying behavior is to recognize what is motivating, what is driving the person to be a bully or to be a mean, cruel person. So, seeing that the person is trying to make you miserable because *he is feeling miserable within himself* is the first step. Recognition is the first step.

UNDERSTANDING

The second step is to understand that he is trying to control your emotional state, trying to make you *feel worse than he feels*. That is his sole goal.

SOVEREIGNTY OF THE MIND

The third step is to realize that your mind is *sovereign* — that is, it stands as a free and independent thinking mind that has "Free Will" and that cannot actually be controlled by anyone or anything. We are only psychologically controlled by others if we *allow* ourselves to be controlled by them. It is a choice that we each make as individuals. Yes, we can be *influenced* by others, but they cannot *control* our thinking. In that way, we are always free and independent thinkers.

I typically prefer to use non-religious language like "sovereignty of the mind" so that all people, whether they are religious or non-religious, may readily understand the concepts I discuss. But for those who are comfortable with religious references, I think this reference from the Civil War movie *The Free State of Jones* speaks directly to the point I'm making.

At the burial ceremony for several of their group who had just been hanged by Confederate soldiers, the movie's main character, Newton Knight (played by Matthew McConaughey) a former Confederate soldier himself, shared the following moving words of inspiration to his band of rebel fighters — a group of former slaves and poor white farmers fighting alongside together — "You cannot own a child of God."

Yes, Knight/McConaughey was referring to slavery. But I would argue that bullying others is a form of attempted slavery. It is, however, always our sovereign choice to allow — or not allow — the bully to "enslave" our minds, our spirits, our hearts. As we've discussed here, the bully may enslave our bodies, but never our minds.

In the case of cruelty, or bullying, or any form of meanness — as in any situation — we retain that control, that ability to choose. And so, we can choose to not be mentally controlled, to not be made to feel miserable by the actions or behavior of another. (We will discuss HOW in the next section.)

Now, granted, this is often difficult to do. It does take a strong mind to make this happen, to make that choice. However, I suggest that it is not as difficult or impossible as we sometimes might think.

And it is a choice we owe to ourselves. How much more intimate a choice is there than to choose actions, thoughts and behavior that acknowledge our self-worth? It's easy to pay lip service to it — jumping up and down in the hotel ballroom while spouting in our umpteenth affirmations workshop that "I am a valuable, powerful, self-sufficient human being," "I deserve to be happy!"

We each do that all too often, and we tend to stop at just saying the affirmations. We need to go further and take action. Because actions speak louder than words.

So, in addition to recognition, understanding cruelty, and having that attitude of sovereignty in our minds, what else can we do?

What affirmative actions can we take?

CONFUSION

Any behavior that is *unexpected* by the person who is inflicting the cruelty, will cause him *confusion*. That is a key step in thwarting his cruelty. Confusion.

For example, laughing or otherwise displaying strength within yourself is unnerving to someone inflicting cruelty. It is not meeting his ends. It does not serve him. You are not being dominated by him, controlled by him. He will not derive happiness from someone who is happier than he is. And in this case, he defines happiness as control. He wants to control you — that gives him happiness. Do not give him that. Maintain your self-control, and you will control his happiness over you.

In other words, if you maintain your self-control, he will be unhappy and will leave you alone or at least will ease up. And when he eases up, that opens up opportunities for you to act and "escape" from the situation, either literally physically or emotionally. Or, even to turn the tables on him.

Ian Fleming's character James Bond honed this skill of

thwarting his cruel captors repeatedly throughout his long fictional lifetime.

Remember, by definition, the cruel person is deriving his happiness from people who are more miserable than he is. If you do not succumb to his efforts to make you miserable, you cause him to fail. He will typically move on to someone much easier than you to make them miserable instead, or at the very least your not succumbing to his efforts will cause him doubt, which will open doors for you to jump through and escape or counter his efforts.

What about *physical pain*?

Because we do live in physical bodies that can be subjected to pain, cruel people will often tend to go there first. However, if we believe and experience that our minds are separate from our bodies, that our minds are sovereign as I said earlier, independent and free-thinking, then this will help us to push through the pain, the physical pain. Which will cause the bully to be confused.

Remember those James Bond torture scenes and how James behaved towards his cruel captors? James was often laughing, joking, verbally going on the offensive aggressively, asking them troubling questions that made the bullies doubt what they were doing.

Again, that is the next step to "transcending the cruelty" of the person inflicting it, namely *causing them confusion*. This unexpected behavior to withstand physical or emotional pain and not allow that very real physical or emotional pain to cause us *mental suffering*, or misery, will disconcert the bully, and in James Bond's situation, the confusion often caused the bully to make a momentary mistake that James took advantage of. Watch for it next time he is captured — he successfully employs this strategy and maneuver time and time again.

Create your own version of James Bond if you are the victim. Think out-of-the-box, cause confusion. Do or say the unexpected.

I acknowledge that this is not an easy task if you are the victim. But, these are the effective steps to thwarting the bully when confronted.

1. Recognition
2. Understanding
3. Sovereignty
4. Confusion
5. Separation

FINAL THOUGHTS

This is the notion of *Transcending Cruelty* and the concept of the *Importance of Being Important*.

How we can recognize bullying, why it occurs, and how to deal with it effectively if it is directed at us, or at those we love.

How these two very important concepts — how understanding them and applying the principles within them — can help improve our quality of life, our state of happiness by reducing our level of suffering, if even just incrementally, by wresting control back from those who may try to push their importance on us.

The Plague Of The Importance Of Being Important

We often hear — in these times of the COVID-19 pandemic — the word "plague."

What does the word "plague" mean?

Webster's Dictionary says: "a disastrous affliction, an epidemic disease causing a high rate of mortality."

I want to take this idea a bit further, outside of the current COVID-19 context. Perhaps to shine a light on a bigger problem, an underlying problem, maybe even a cause of the "psychological plague" that has infected the human race for millennia and continues to wreak havoc among us today.

THE "IMPORTANCE OF BEING IMPORTANT"

First let's start by briefly addressing some commonly discussed psycho-social ills that we all have seen that afflict our species.

I think most of us would agree that bias exists in our world. "Bias" means preference. Plain and simple. It comes in many forms.

Height. Weight. Economic. Health. Race. Ethnicity. Age. Gender. Sexual preference. Nationality. City. Rural. Sports team. University. High School. Company. Diet. Eye color. Hair color. Baldness. Vocal. Quiet. The list could go on.

You get the idea. We are all biased about something.

And it is not inherently a bad thing. I would argue it is necessary to make assessments. To discriminate in life. That's what "discrimination" used to mean before the U.S. culture labeled that word negatively in the 1960's when it became almost exclusively associated with racial prejudice.

So bias — as preference — is real. Necessary. And not bad by itself.

What is bad is when we ignore our biases. When we become unconscious to them. And we act indiscriminately without forethought. And when those biases become hurtful to others.

When I was in elementary school, the "mentally challenged" kids were intermingled with all of us in gym class and during recess, i.e., play time before school and after lunch. Some kids would tease them and make fun of them. I would intervene. Tell those kids to stop. To leave them alone. And I would talk with the challenged kids sometimes — publicly and privately — so they knew they were also "like us" and not just different due to their mental abilities. I would do it so the other kids could see me too.

It is not that I didn't see those kids as different mentally. Of course I did. And it's not that I didn't prefer to play with my other friends. Of course I did. But I drew the line when I saw hurtful behavior directed at them. I did not allow that in my presence. And whenever I could, I found a way to include them in our schoolyard games.

We cannot control the thinking and actions of others. But when in the presence of bad behavior, we can act. Or not. That is a choice we each have.

So bias is real. But how we handle our biases is up to each of us.

Another example from my youth... When I lived and worked teaching meditation in Asia in my 20's, I many times observed racial bias. I had previously personally experienced it growing up in a Caucasian-dominated Boston suburb. But in

Asia it was different.

I observed Caucasians being treated negatively by the dominant Asian culture. This was a brand new experience for me. And it was very apparent — not hidden at all — that it was simply because the Caucasians were racially not Asian. The Asians saw them as lesser.

It was apparent both in the disdain, the sometimes outright visible look of contempt on the face of the Chinese or Koreans I lived among when they interacted with some American, British or Australian Caucasians. And it was verbally apparent in what they called them — translation from Chinese — "white foreign devils."

Now, please understand I'm not here to get into a political colonialism discussion. That's not my point. Because I have also witnessed many instances of justified anger by the colonized Asian cultures.

So what's my point?

The tribalism.

The separation that humans do when they are in groups. It exists worldwide.

And why do we do it in a way that is sometimes hurtful to others?

I think we are all — yes ALL of us — without exception — sometimes afflicted with the "Importance of Being Important."

And we use it — usually unconsciously — when we feel tired, disempowered or insecure.

Why?

Because it makes us feel good.

Why did some kids bully the mentally challenged kids at the Cleveland Elementary School in Norwood, Massachusetts in 1960? Because it made them feel powerful, "better than someone else."

Why did the Chinese shop owners snicker behind the backs of the much wealthier (arguably more powerful) Caucasian women and men, and talk about them negatively in Cantonese so they wouldn't understand? Because it made them feel more powerful, "better than someone else."

At least temporarily.

And so we go on. And on. And on. We repeat that behavior for generations and generations. We teach our children by our behavior and they, in turn, teach their children.

And these scenarios are repeated worldwide hundreds of millions of times a day.

Every day. Every year.

In every culture.

We as a human race need to stop and think about this tribal mentality — the "group think" of manipulating various biases towards others to make us feel good. Think and reflect on this behavioral pattern we have created for ourselves worldwide for the past 400,000 years. Resist and reject it when encouraged by our political or religious leaders to act in that tribal way.

And especially when that tribalism leads to cruelty.

"Cruelty" is when someone gets pleasure out of hurting another person.

And why do they act cruelly? For the same reason we discussed above. Because they feel weaker, more insecure, less powerful at that moment. And by demeaning someone else, we make them feel worse so we feel better.

It could be caused simply by fatigue or low blood sugar — I have had moments like that when I snapped at my kids unnecessarily when I was exhausted or too hungry from driving too long without a break. We have all had moments like that.

Or in a more complicated psychological profile, the

insecurity could be deeper and less transient, perhaps caused by the powerlessness and lack of love shown a child by a father especially in the child's formative years. Even maybe resulting in such a lack of sensibility for the needs of others that the "Importance of Being Important" and its cruelty component causes sociopathic behavior in the child later as an adult.

These general principles of the "Importance of Being Important" and "Transcending Cruelty" were introduced in the 30thNovember talk I organized in 2014. And they are topics that the spiritual group, known as the Movement, that some of you may have heard me discuss in my classes, has encouraged us to discuss further.

In conclusion — and to be continued — because this is a long term discussion that I hope will continue among us for millennia worldwide — bias or preference is real. I would argue it is neutral, neither positive nor negative. But when our biases become exercised in a hurtful way — perhaps instigated by our need for the "Importance of Being Important" to satiate our insecurities — then that cruel behavior needs to be curbed by providing the means to develop more inner security.

While the list of experts to provide more security in the economic, political, educational, gender equality, and other arenas is long, I am not one of them. So instead, I focus on my work helping people in my areas of expertise — how to "turn within" and strengthen ourselves from the inside out, learning how to think more clearly and develop practical life skills, and Overcoming the Fear of Death.

I ask you to look at your areas of expertise — whether professionally or avocationally — and apply your energies as you see fit to helping others develop greater inner security. In that way, you will be a contributor and solution provider to what I would argue is the most debilitating plague of the human race — the Importance of Being Important.

For Guys Only

I'm a guy.

I've played organized competitive sports, led large business organizations, and scuba dived at 115 feet deep in the open ocean.

But those of you who measure "being a guy" only in those terms are missing out. Not only that, but you could be setting a bad example for your young sons, the men of the future.

Too many guys measure their "maleness" by how macho they are. By how much testosterone they can exude to the world — typically to the world of women. How much of that male hormone they can spill onto the widest variety of playing fields — in business, sports, and yes, at home — any number of what they view as the "battlefields" of life.

Ok, I don't want to leave out my LBGTQ friends from this discussion because yes, those guys are guilty of limiting themselves in this way too. They also can be equally guilty of excessive "peacock feather rattling." And yes, they too can be fathers to straight or gay sons. So, being as inclusive as possible....

We guys — all of us — need to grow up.
We need to emotionally mature beyond puberty.

Because not only are we potentially missing out, but we're also creating a higher likelihood of bad hurtful behavior towards others. And that includes others whom we may care about.

What are we "missing out" on?

How about having a mutually loving, emotionally rich relationship with our spouse or girlfriend? Or with our children? Or our grandchildren? (Yes, grandpa, it's never too late to start moving beyond your puberty-based fears and limitations...)

By continuing to act in that emotionally "me-oriented" state we embraced as 16-year olds, we limit ourselves to women (or men) who will "put up with us." As opposed to partners who actually want to be with us, and feel like they can thrive *with* us. Not in spite of us.

And worse. That juvenile narcissistic behavior, when played out by a 40, 50, or 60-year old man — or god forbid, if he is a father — risks hurting others through his bullying, of his spouse or children.

And then, what a tragic example of how to "be a man" such a dad demonstrates to his sons.

While we're on the subject of dads, the "I am who I am because of my father" is a poor excuse in my book. We each can change. If we want to. If we are strong enough.

That's strength. True strength.

When you are met with adversity — in this case maybe a lousy role model — and you nevertheless overcome the bullying behavior of your father and become a truly strong, emotionally caring human being. A better father than what you had.

That is a demonstration of *true strength*.

So guys, no matter how young or old you are, or where you live in the world, think about this.

Honestly ask yourself if this describes you. And know that you can do something about it, if you want. You can change. You can grow. You can be a better person — you can let your testosterone flow and be a caring guy too. You can be "stronger" in a real way — not just a showy peacock way.

And you might find that your girlfriend, spouse, or kids may love you more for it.

That's the benefit of being a real man. Not just a man respected by men.

But a man respected by women.

And children.

The Art Of Boxing —
The Physical Versus The
Non-Physical

I'm watching a boxing movie, "Southpaw" right now as I'm writing this essay. And Forest Whitaker just said to Jake Gyllenhaal, "boxing's not about this (punching) — boxing's about this…" (pointing to his head).

The non-physical, *not* the physical.

The problem on our planet as human beings is we forget that basic principle. We get caught up in the physical so much so that we ignore and eventually completely forget about the non-physical — the mind, thinking, attitudes that form our behavior and affect our physical life.

Just like Forest Whitaker as the boxing trainer pointed out to Jake Gyllenhaal, my role on the planet this lifetime is to remind us not to forget that basic principle.

That's not to say that we ignore the physical. We just must remember that it does not start with the physical. It starts with the mental, the non-physical.

And when we remember that, we can then begin the long journey of understanding our minds better — more deeply — its complexity more profoundly.

COMFORT AND FAMILIARITY WITH OUR OWN MINDS

I think this is one of the main reasons why most people fear death. Their experience of their minds is basic, *not* profound, *not* open to the complexity of the mental possibilities of human experience. We tend to be very comfortable with a relatively small portion of our mind, what I sometimes refer to as "the supermarket aisle" mind that each of us uses regularly on a daily basis — the "Do I need peanut butter, olives, milk today?" ...the decision-making part of our mind.

Don't get me wrong. It's an important part of our mind — it keeps us from bumping into walls, and getting into accidents driving our car through busy intersections. But it represents only a tiny portion of our minds.

The rest of the mind that tends not to be used, all the various channels and avenues of mental experience that are also possible for each of us to experience — our innate intuitive capabilities and especially our ability to sense and experience the unseen beyond the physical world — tend to go completely unnoticed by us, and therefore unexercised.

And therefore, when we have experiences in those areas of our minds, maybe triggered by a drug, hypnotism, Near-Death Experience (NDE), or some other external stimulus (yes, an NDE is an experience "external" to one's essential self), the experience is so unfamiliar to us, that a feeling of being "out-of-control" often dominates our awareness, may even overwhelm us — meaning, it is so unlike the "supermarket aisle mind"... so unlike the physical control we seem to have over our bodies — that we experience confusion and sometimes deep anxiety, perhaps even trauma, as a result.

It's just like the boxer who has entered the ring physically prepared, but mentally unprepared. And when something does *not* go according to plan, when something unexpected happens, the boxer is overwhelmed and confused. Relying merely on his/her physical skills is not enough.

THE SOLUTION

So, what's the solution?

Whether we are literally or figuratively a boxer, if we

practice "turning within" on a regular basis through some effortless form of meditation or other inward mental process, we can open our awareness gradually to a wide range of previously unknown areas of our minds. And by doing this in a *natural* way — without using artificially-created external stimulants (drugs or other means) — the nervous system *automatically* self-regulates, can adjust and acclimate comfortably to the new experiences of the mind in a balanced way.

And in this process, it will develop a familiarity with them so that when we do experience them again — perhaps in an OBE (out-of-body experience), NDE, or even in death itself — our minds will be so open, so aware and awake, and moreover so *familiar* with these various other avenues that exist within it, that there will be no fear, no anxiety, no feeling of "being out of control."

Because by then, we will have experienced enough of a comfort level with those experiences that they no longer feel overwhelming — or foreign.

So, getting comfortable with the non-physical starts with recognizing that the physical is only a part of our reality — it is not the "be all and end all." As easy as it is to get distracted — even seduced — by all the flashing lights, pyrotechnics, smells, tastes and touches of physical reality, we must not forget that fact.

And thus, while the physical and non-physical most certainly "share the stage" in our lives here as humans, the non-physical is ultimately what is crucial for the quality of our experience. The mind, in other words, is where that starts.

For us to be successful as a boxer, it starts between our ears, so to speak. It starts in our mind, our attitude, our understanding. And from there, our physical abilities become honed and effective. That's how we become effective boxers.

That's how we become effective "livers of life" in physical bodies on planet Earth.

Spiritual Materialism

*Materialism is usually talked about
in the context of money, owning property, amassing wealth.
Let's look at how it is equally present
in the world of spirituality.*

Many religions and spiritual pursuits use the classic "carrot" as the incentive to motivate their seekers and believers into following those groups' beliefs and schools of thought.

"If you follow these rules, you'll go to Heaven."

"If you meditate and follow this lifestyle — wear these clothes, beads, shave your head, be celibate — you will reach Nirvana or Enlightenment," etc.

I would say that this is no different than someone luring someone in by promising a fancy car or a fancy new house, a new castle, a new estate to live in.

I have written in my first book about my friend Charlie who is now a philosophy professor with whom I taught meditation many decades ago. Charlie created this quite simple but ingenious model to describe people's experience. It's what he called the "Conscious of XYZ" model.

He would say that most people focus their experience on the XYZ's, the objects of experience, the "things" that are definable, specific, identifiable — the car, the home, the money, the clothes, or in the case of the spiritual, the lifestyle and promise of "enlightenment." Conversely, they don't focus their attention, nor are most people even aware of, the "conscious" side of the model — the fact that we have to be conscious to even have experience, that we need a mind to experience. Most of us get so caught up in the XYZ's that we "identify" ourselves with them, we define ourselves by our XYZ's.

So, in this model, the "carrots" that we are caught up in... whether they be BMWs, castles, or even "higher states of consciousness"…are all XYZ's. They are identifiable objects to be sought out. Instead of living life moment to moment, in the present, we prioritize our lives in such a way that we will do everything it takes, everything possible to reach those goals.

But are those goals that we really want to aim for?

What are "higher states of consciousness" that so many meditation students seek and that some sell all their worldly possessions to try to realize? Are they real? Are they worth all that sacrifice?

"Enlightenment" or "Nirvana" is reputed to be the goal of many spiritual practices. It is described as some sort of state of perfection, something akin to "living Heaven on Earth." Bliss. Ultimate Fulfillment. A utopian psycho-emotional spiritual state of mind.

But is enlightenment "forever" as it is promised? Is it permanent and never changing? Or does it just describe different colorations and experiences that we may have in our waking, dreaming and sleeping states?

We can debate this issue. But for me what's important is not whether these concepts are their own "states of consciousness" or whether they are merely colorations and experiences of waking, dreaming or sleeping.

What matters is *how we treat them.*

Are we so enamored of them that we drop everything, forsake our friendships and relationships, or worse...do we compromise our ethics because we espouse "the ends justify the means"?

For example, do you lie, or "bend the truth," to promote fundraisers for your spiritual guru?

For me, this is where the "rubber meets the road." This is where the purported seeker "would-be-saint" is tested.

Does she or he take the bait?

This is where many falter. And I think it's primarily because they have put this spiritual goal in the XYZ category. It has become for them a goal, an object to possess. By doing so, that spiritual experience has then become no different than the desire to own the fancy BMW.

It has become a thing.

And for many seekers it becomes a thing with which *they measure themselves and others.* "How enlightened are you?" "Am I more enlightened than they are?"

These are red flags. They are signs that person has lost perspective.

That they have become a *spiritual materialist.*

And what about remembering past lives? Is it a sign of some higher development, some alleged higher state of consciousness?

I think not.

I think those memories can sometimes come more easily to some than others because of many factors. Primarily a lesser state of fear about the distant past. Combined with an attitude about what they've done which is not blocked by some strong distaste from a past experience — guilt, shame, embarrassment, pain, to name a few common blockers.

In other words, I think our emotional reactions to experience can leave an imprint in us that can block our ability to easily access our memories. Psychologists tell us this happens to us *in this life* — some people, for example, don't remember their childhood, anything before they were, say, 10 years old. So why couldn't the same reason explain why we block our even older memories?

At any rate, whatever the reason, I think there may be many factors that contribute to our having difficulty remembering past life experiences.

But more importantly, to our discussion here — It should not be taken as an indication of that individual's so-called level of evolution or degree of self-awareness.

I think judging ourselves and others by such metrics is also a form of spiritual materialism. We are using essentially a "thing," an "object of experience" — whether someone remembers something or not — to judge another person's level of self-awareness.

Moreover, I don't think anyone can judge another person's level of self-awareness. I don't think any of us can even judge *our own* level of self-awareness with any degree of accuracy. Because, as I often say: "As compared to what?" — "...as measured against what?"

I don't think there is any absolute yardstick out there in the universe.

So what are we comparing ourselves to? Essentially we are comparing ourselves to ourselves. And that's as far as it goes I think.

And if that's the case, then I think we just need to focus on living our lives. Enjoying our lives, living in the present.

Just get on with it.

Stop wasting our time trying to assess ourselves, critique ourselves, measure ourselves against others, or against other people's supposed yardsticks that either they or some group or some organization has created, typically "out of whole cloth" — i.e., totally fabricated, made up.

I'm a pragmatist. It is simply not productive. And arguably, it is inaccurate.

Now, can certain experiences we have inform us about

ourselves, tell us more about what makes us tick, why we do certain things, why we are attracted to certain experiences?

Absolutely.

So is there value in looking at experiences, talking about them, understanding them in order to understand ourselves better — whether they be related to self-awareness type experiences, or our past life memories?

Yes.

However, that does not mean that they are a "measurement" of us in any way. Not of our intelligence, nor our wisdom, nor of our level of self-awareness or spiritual growth.

They are experiences, plain and simple.

So we should treat them as such, use them as such, to help us learn more about ourselves. But not to measure ourselves or to measure others. That is a waste of time.

Using them to understand ourselves better helps us live a happier, more productive life now in the present. Without dwelling in the past or getting overly enamored by some experience that is fleeting by its very nature.

This is where the seeker should spend his or her valuable life energy.

Focusing on knowing themselves more fully, not merely by "turning within" through meditation, but also by paying attention and learning from their actions, emotional reactions, and insights into the choices they make...i.e., how they live their lives.

So, if the seeker chooses to be effective at seeking greater knowledge of him or herself, perhaps they should choose "spiritual insightfulness" over spiritual materialism.

Sex & Spirituality

To be clear, this essay does not address the issue of power and sex, or non-consensual sex, which is a different topic that I cover in my essays on Cruelty. Power — whether emotionally, physically, or intellectually — over another in order to get happiness by causing them suffering or pain is "cruel" behavior. Clearly, that is not spiritual behavior.

In this essay, we are talking about consensual sex among adults, where neither person is pushing their power over the other.

Lots of people are good at being sexual, but how many people can be sexual when they are "being good"?

How many people between the ages of 18 and 99 do you know who would like to have more sex? Maybe they would say, as much sex as possible. Some might even say, all the time...

OK, maybe not everyone has that level of appetite, but I'm pretty sure that most people on the planet would have a lot more sex if they didn't feel burdened by their various beliefs and other restricting factors.

Let's talk about some of those beliefs and see whether they make sense or not.

OUR BELIEFS ABOUT SEX

So, what stops most people from having as much sex as they'd like?

Most people would say things like — STDs, pregnancy, various beliefs about it being "socially unacceptable," or even "against one's religious beliefs." Some might even believe celibacy is more spiritual, that it conserves "life energy."

To be clear, I'm *not* here to promote indiscriminate sex, violating marital vows, or ignoring safe sex guidelines.

I am here, however, to discuss *the guilt or negative thoughts, or limiting beliefs* often associated with sex. I also want to explore some alternative perspectives on sex itself.

Here we go...

IS SEX WRONG?

Why is sex considered "bad" or "wrong" by some people? Taboo?

Aside from the possible health-related reasons that a percentage of our society may legitimately have regarding sex, the most widespread source of negative views about sex seems to be from various religious beliefs. And these beliefs are not isolated to any particular cultures or scriptures — they are worldwide.

These beliefs have been passed down for generations, for thousands of years — they have influenced our great grandparents and parents, as well as our world's political leaders, and our advertising agencies and movie moguls. And therefore, these beliefs have influenced many country's laws and cultural norms — and ultimately, our personal relationships.

WHO STARTED THIS THINKING THAT SEX IS WRONG, "LESSER"?

Many different religions have long-held beliefs that it is "more spiritual, more godly" to spend as much time thinking about or devoting one's life efforts to seeking God. That celibacy was the ideal.

I think this is because many of the originators of that thinking came from more 'reclusive lives' — perhaps even as monks or nuns in the Western traditions, or as yogis and gurus in the Eastern traditions. Their life choices dictated that they divorced themselves from physical sexual activity, and over time I think they developed a negative attitude towards it — a view that it was somehow "lesser" than their spiritual choice to be celibate — that by being celibate, they could more quickly and effectively be "closer to God," or "become Enlightened."

That was their belief.

Very few of them chose the "householder" lifestyle of having a family with children, and all the responsibilities that go along with that choice (arguably a much more difficult road in life to navigate than sitting quietly in a cave, monastery or convent being fed and cared for by the local devotees...but I digress). As a result, their experience base became more and more limited over the many generations of monks, nuns, yogis, and gurus who came through those various traditions. And with each passing generation of reclusive celibates came more and more justification for the sex-free lifestyle they had each chosen. To them, having sex and having relationships with the opposite sex was a distraction from their focus on "being with God," towards "seeking Enlightenment."

So, you see, it all makes sense. I think it's explainable as a choice they made for seemingly good reasons at the time, not only because they believed it was good for themselves, but also because — by extension — they believed it was good for us. But we need to also recognize that they were in their own small universe, talking only among themselves reinforcing a limited range of life experience. They were self-referential. "Drinking their own Kool Aid," so to speak.

So, instead, let's imagine we had never heard of their beliefs about sex, and let's think about this ourselves, for ourselves. Does it make sense to view sex as inherently good or bad — spiritually speaking?

MAYBE SEX IS NEUTRAL

I think sex itself is neutral. What I mean by that is that sex itself is not "loaded" emotionally, spiritually, or psychologically all by itself.

It is a physical act through which procreation occurs, the continuation of the species is ensured. We, however, tend to *associate* various emotions and content with it — both good and bad — "he or she loves me (or at least is attracted to me...!!)," "too much sex is slutty," etc. But those are associations that we do from within the social norms of our respective cultures — absent that, sex itself is largely a neutral act — especially from a spiritual perspective.

JIMMY CHOO STILETTOS

It is analogous to going to shop for a new pair of Jimmy Choo shoes. For some women, that act may simply be a neutral act — merely a shopping task on their To Do List.

OK...maybe that's a small percentage of our Western urban culture's female population...!! But, for other women (and yes, for some of us men who are comfortable shopping for our women), shopping for new Jimmy Choo stilettos is an emotionally stimulating, almost 'religious' experience eliciting pleasure responses from a whole host of sensors.

So, see what I mean?

Much of what we do in life are mere acts to which we attach and associate certain emotionally-charged experience. But, in a vacuum, the act is merely an act, a process. In this case, buying a pair of shoes.

I think sex is largely the same.

And therefore, I think a good starting point would be for us all to view sex as neutral — and most importantly, "Guilt-Free." Again, not to be irresponsible in our actions or relationships at all, but to be free from any guilt *of having sex.*

No spiritual guilt around sex.

"HOW" — NOT JUST THE "WHAT"

Instead of looking at sex through the guilt lens — the "right or wrong" lens, as is often done — let's look at it through the lens of "Personal Choice." I think this is a much healthier way of looking at sex.

Some may choose to engage in being very sexually active. Others may not. Those are choices that need to be respected, since Free Will is the most important aspect of our being "self-aware minds," in my opinion.

And, most important within the concept of Personal Choice is "The HOW," not just "The WHAT."

In other words, I think *our intent* is key, and while merely having a good intention is not good enough by itself — i.e., actions and their results do matter — when all things are equal, when the actions are basically the same, the intent behind them becomes critical to look at.

For example, in dating, breaking up is a common process that couples go through. But, "How" they break up — i.e., the process and *how they treat each other* within that process — is critical. Is there an intent to hurt the other person? True — in a break-up, often one or both parties get hurt. But, is there an *intent to hurt,* and moreover is there an *intent to lessen the hurting* of the other as much as possible?

And with sex in that dating relationship, it is no different. How we treat our partner in the process of dating that leads up to having sex, through the act of having sex and afterwards is critically important to how we assess ourselves and how we are assessed by others as respectful spiritually-minded, kind lovers. Hot sex does not mean disrespectful, hurtful, narcissistic sex.

Those are factors I think we need to look at more closely when assessing how "spiritual" we are in our dealings with others.

111

Not just looking at the "What," but also inspecting the "How."

CAN SEX BE MORE THAN NEUTRAL?

Although having sex may be largely a neutral process, can it be more than that? Can it be more of a positive experience — in a physical, emotional *and* even a spiritual way?

I think it definitely can be…

- A source of physical pleasure
- A way to relax, release stress, improve sleep
- A way to release endorphins
- A way to let go and 'surrender oneself' completely (albeit momentarily)
- A means of connection with another — emotionally, mentally, spiritually

SPIRITUAL SEX

So…what about "Spiritual Sex"…is it an oxymoron or is it something we can aspire to and experience in our daily lives?

We've listed above several ways for us to experience sex in more than a neutral way — in the various ways we can experience sex as a positive experience without hurting others.

Let's focus now on the last one we discussed — sex as a means of "connecting" with another person, because ultimately I think connection both with ourselves and with others is the essence of what spirituality is about.

MORE THAN THE TRADITIONAL VIEW OF "SPIRITUAL CONNECTION"

This is where I depart from most writers and thinkers about sex. I see sex as a vehicle through which we can experience the FULL RANGE of connection — mentally, emotionally, physically — on *all* levels.

Those who may be more attuned to language in the many spiritual schools worldwide use terms like "chakras," "energies," etc. They typically view sex as a lower chakra, a lower energy experience. And sometimes, if there is a very special connection between the sexual partners, they may view sex as a higher energy experience.

I say No — it does not have to be an "either-or" proposition. It *can* be BOTH.

In fact, I see it as possibly even more than that.

I see sex as a possible vehicle for ALL connection — through all levels of chakras. Not just the so-called "higher energies"... the higher chakras...nor just the lower chakras. But through the many thousands of chakras in our bodies. This experience of being able to access and experience *any and all* of the chakras and energy centers throughout the body during sex is what I would redefine as "spiritual."

Spiritual sex.

It can be experienced as a pulsating of the energies through the entire body and energy centers, not just during sexual climax, but throughout the act of having sex. Some have labeled it a kundalini experience, but I choose to use more neutral, non-cultural language and just call it a pulsating energy flow that can occur. Very physical, yet energetic as well.

And with the right partner, the experience can be a catalyst for connection and healing — a breadth and depth of connection that is seldom experienced with another person.

You know the expression, "The whole is more than the sum of the parts."

CHOOSING SPIRITUAL SEX

I think, in the end, it can be a choice, a personal choice we can make, perhaps even just through our intention to make it so. And, if our experience of "turning within" has been effective and we have developed a strong connectedness within ourselves, then we can translate and seemingly transfer that energy and connectedness out to others — in this case, with our sexual partner.

This would truly be "spiritual sex" — a liberating experience and at the same time an intimate connecting experience both with oneself and one's partner.

Extremely physical from the root energy centers through the heart center and embracing the ethereal — in sequence and all at once. That is what is possible.

FINAL THOUGHTS

Most people experience sex simply as physical connection. Some experience it as emotional connection. And a few people experience it as spiritual connection with oneself and the other person.

But, ultimately, everyone experiences it as some form of *connection*. This is where I think the emphasis should be.

Connection with oneself and with others is where life happens. Looking at sex as yet *another vehicle* through which to experience human life would significantly enrich and enhance the relationships of people worldwide.

After all, isn't it our relationships throughout our life that really mean the most to us?

When people are on their deathbed, it's not all their cars, houses, jobs and money that they have (or don't have) that flash through their mind and are most important to them at that moment. It's their loved ones, their friends, their teammates, their colleagues, who are the most important to them in the end. Their friendships, their relationships.

So, why wait 'til you're on your deathbed to enrich and explore...and cherish those relationships?

We all need to start *now*.

And, while I'm not suggesting that everyone go out and have indiscriminate sex with strangers, I am recommending that we take another look at how we view sex. I am strongly recommending that we look at sex as another vehicle through which we can *connect in many ways* with another human being.

And that we come at this with respect, kindness, and without guilt.

Following The Path Of Imperfection

I wrote this to address the age-old question of the seeker who seeks perfection in life, the meditation student who all too often sits at the feet (whether literally or figuratively) of his/her guru in a master-disciple relationship of subservience and unquestioning obedience...

Remember this...

No one is perfect.

Not you. Not me. Not any teacher or guru.

Here's why.

Every mind or soul is eternal. At least that's what I think based on my experiences so far. But even if it's not, it's around for a very, very long time — long enough that it might as well be "eternal."

And as such, our mind or soul can always be growing and learning more about itself. If that's true, then no static (unchanging) state of perfection can ever exist. It is an illusory goal.

But, why do we so often and so quickly latch onto this notion of perfection as a goal?

Because we are insecure. We want the perceived anchor of having a goal that is a "landing spot." We think that having a goal like that will make us feel secure.

But does it really?

What happens when that goal begins to not match up with our reality of life, with our actual daily experience?

For example, what if our stated goal of perfection says things to us like, "*When you are truly fulfilled, you are always happy" or, "When you are aligned with your life purpose, then everything that you need in your life materializes effortlessly..."*

Sounds good, right? Reassuring? Definitely.

But what if no matter how much you devote your mental, emotional, physical, and spiritual energy and effort to this seemingly high-minded purposeful objective, you feel like you fall short? That no matter how hard you try, and no matter how clear your intention is, nothing is ever perfect, and sometimes you are unhappy.

Then you feel like you've failed. You've failed yourself.

Or so you think.

But think about it. Have you really failed, or have you set yourself up for failure *at the start* by seeking a goal that is *never* attainable?

I think it's the latter.

In fact, I think such a goal often *promotes suffering.*

Albeit unintentional — it's an unintended consequence. Because the reality of life is that we all experience imperfections in our lives. And if we assess ourselves based on a yardstick of perfection, we set ourselves up for failure, unhappiness and despair.

Instead, I suggest an alternative approach: ongoing "learning" through the *acceptance of our imperfections.*

SELF-LOVE

Said differently, this can be an opportunity for "self-love."

What do I mean by that?

It's easy to say, "Love yourself" when everything is going smoothly. It's not so easy when things are far less than perfect. That is the true test of one's self-love.

Can you accept and "love" all those things about yourself that you aren't fond of? That you see as "imperfect" — whether they be physical, mental, or emotional?

117

And honesty is important. It's critical.

Double talk is unacceptable. For example, saying that you (or your guru) took that action *"merely in order to teach you a lesson"* is double talk, plain and simple. How about instead accepting that life is imperfect and that it's okay to make mistakes and that they're *not* a sign of weakness, lower consciousness, or anything "lesser"?

Might that attitude and understanding contribute to more happiness and contentment, and less self-criticism in us? Less suffering?

Definitely.

FINAL THOUGHTS

So, when you hear yourself "following" that part of yourself (or a guru) that is looking for a sense of perfection, perhaps for comfort and support, recognize that it's a red flag. It's a sign that you may need to "go within," be honest with yourself, watch out for double talk, and be okay with the feeling of discomfort that often comes along with what we can simply call..."living life."

The sublime and stabilizing feeling of "being content within oneself" *can* come as a direct result of "turning within," Knowing Oneself more deeply, and accepting *all* aspects of oneself — *regardless* of how well they align with *other* people's value systems of development, evolution, or enlightenment.

So...

If a guru comes into your life and says:

"Follow me, I will show you the path to Perfection...," instead of selling all your worldly possessions, quitting your job, and leaving your family for a life of obedience at his or her ashram in the mountains, you might just smile and say:

"Thanks but no thanks.
I'm having fun finding my way along the Path of Imperfection,
and I like making my own infinite choices just fine."

Self-Interest

What is self-interest? Self-interest is similar to self-care, but it is more innate. Self-interest is "built in." Self-care needs to be learned and be acted upon.

SELFISHNESS

When one's self-interest becomes so dominant that it is at the exclusion of all others' interests to the point of harming them, emotionally, mentally or physically. That is being selfish.

ACKNOWLEDGE & MONITOR

So we need to first acknowledge that we each have self-interest. That it exists as a natural — and emotionally and morally "neutral" — state of mind. Arguably it is a critically important, life sustaining element of every mind. Of every individual consciousness. So we need to discard any negative labels that we may have incorrectly associated with being self-interested. That is step #1.

And then we each need to monitor our own mind's innate tendencies of self-interest. To ensure that we don't stray into the "selfish" range — because that's what it is, a range, not a black and white line — where we either consciously engage in hurting others by our selfishness, our excessive self interest, or where we unconsciously hurt others through our laziness or negligence, our lack of self awareness about our thoughts and actions.

SELF-ABSORBED

Finally, those who have allowed — maybe even encouraged — themselves to become excessively selfish human beings we call "self-absorbed" people. Absorbed with their own self-interest to such a degree as to not care whether they hurt others in the process. And who may even gain happiness and enjoyment from hurting others — the very definition of "cruelty" towards other people.

We also call such people "narcissists."

So, as you can see, it's more of a spectrum of how the human mind thinks and chooses. It's not as black and white as some may lead you to believe.

And it's reparable.

HOW THEY INTERRELATE

The farther you may move towards the narcissistic end of the spectrum, the harder it is to balance yourself more towards the neutral state of being self-interested. But most of us hover more in the middle range. And if we become aware of how this is in fact a range, we can make better conscious choices about how we both view ourselves as individuals and how our behavior affects those we interact with.

If we recognize and embrace that we are all self-interested — innately as part of the inherent structure of our minds, then we can actually use that knowledge to enhance our relationships with others, in the following way. If we can identify their self-interests, and we are successful at helping them meet those interests, we will bring happiness to them. And by doing so, we will indirectly bring greater happiness to ourselves.

Suppose my life partner wants to get her therapy practice running as efficiently as possible so she can focus solely on what she loves and is gifted at — counseling her clients. If I can help her hire a great billing person, that act will directly assist her in meeting both her business and emotional interests. And she'll be elated, which in turn will inure to my benefit because by helping her meet that interest, I will have brought her happiness, lessened her stress, and in turn, deepened our relationship bond.

It's not complicated. But it starts by first acknowledging that we are all self-interested, followed by identifying other people's self-interests. Then deciding if those self-interests align enough with ours. And if so, helping them make their self-interested goals a reality.

I say align "enough" because not every alignment is so perfect as in my above therapy practice example.

But, 70-80% alignment is probably heavenly and 60% is acceptable. However, 30-40% is likely unacceptable.

For example, just because you see that a powerful leader has a self-interest that aligns with your own religious, economic or social goals does not mean you automatically help him meet his interests. You need to ask yourself, "How is he planning on meeting those goals?" "Is he taking the 'crush everyone in our way' — sometimes called in litigation the 'scorched earth' — approach to accomplishing those goals?" Does he have "the ends justify the means" belief system? Cheat, lie, steal — it doesn't matter?

Then you might decide that is insufficient alignment for you to support that person's self-interests...regardless of how fervently he supports your religious, economic or social goals.

On the other hand, perhaps your wife really wants to go on a day trip to a place that you both enjoy visiting. But you would rather stay home and watch the football game. What do you do?

Whose self-interest comes out on top in this scenario? Do you view it as "her" interest versus "my" interest? A win-lose competition? You certainly can choose to look at it that way. And you may decide, using that lens, that you're going to be "selfless" and go on the day trip with her. You may choose to sublimate your desires in favor of hers.

That's the "either/or" view of the scenario. Which is not incorrect, of course. There is no right or wrong here.

But I think a slightly different way of looking at that choice may be more self-sustaining for ourselves, in this case the husband.

Why not instead say to oneself, "My love of my wife makes me so happy — arguably a lot happier than staying home and watching a football game — that I'm going with her on the day trip!"

This is probably the unconscious calculus that's going on in your mind. A weighing of the options. And a decision.

But why not make it a conscious articulation inside? I have found there is additional power in the conscious articulation of my choice in such a situation…not making it into a justification, but actually genuinely emotionally feeling that way inside myself, and then acknowledging it.

So, okay. You can call that "selfless" if it makes you feel better. But I see it differently. I see it as your choosing a different way to make yourself happy — perhaps even an overlap of interests (hers and yours) — meeting your self-interest of seeking happiness — that INCLUDES another human being. In this case, arguably the most important human being in your life, besides yourself.

And what a life sustaining — and yes, relationship sustaining — choice it is!

To me, seeing this choice through that different lens brings clarity to our thoughts and actions, and perhaps sets us up for greater ease and spontaneity going forward when making such gray area life choices.

Self-Interested Versus Self-Centered

Could therein be both the cause and solution to the world's problems on this planet?

In fact, that may be where "the rubber meets the road" — the distinction between being self-*interested* and self-*centered*.

Let's unbundle this — one of the most widespread human inner conflicts.

SELF-INTERESTED

I think we are all self-interested. Meaning we look out for our own needs, our own interests. What matters to us. I think that's not only normal and natural. But most importantly, it's necessary.

After all, if I didn't get food and shelter for myself, who else would? On a basic survival level, I wouldn't survive if I didn't look out for myself. My needs.

And not just my basic physical needs for survival. I need to look out for and try to meet my mental and emotional needs as well. Because we are not merely physical beings. We are mental, emotional, and arguably, spiritual beings in physical bodies.

So, someone needs to be the primary caretaker and gatherer of those needs. And that someone is each of us. For each of us.

That makes logical sense. Right?

And in my opinion, this is important to recognize. Because if we recognize and accept that each of us is self-interested in this way that I've described — that it is a normal, natural tendency we all have — then we can be more conscious and intentional about looking out for the needs that *others* around us may have. Recognize *their* interests. And perhaps *help them* meet those needs and interests.

By doing so, we would support that other person, and nurture and cultivate our relationship with them. By helping them be happier. And "what goes around, comes around." Right?

If they're happier, we're happier. It's a win-win.

SELF-CENTERED = "SELFISH"

However, if we are unable to be self-aware enough to see that potential asset — that potentially relationship-altering perspective — then our relationship will likely fall into disrepair.

Because that lack of self-awareness will probably push our neutral self-interested state of mind "over the (proverbial) line" to being *self-centered*. What I am suggesting is that when we become *excessively* self-interested, we become self-centered. And when that happens, we become *selfish*.

Isolated

Alone

We have moved off the neutral state of being self-interested to the negative, energy-draining state of being self-centered. We have become "selfish."

Lonely

We lose our connection with others. Because we have lost our connection *within ourselves*.

"TURNING WITHIN"

By "turning within" and connecting within ourselves, we naturally "feed" ourselves from the inside. It's the basis for giving ourselves life sustaining energy, the ultimate in self-care.

First we must "fill ourselves up." Then we can begin to develop a more complete perspective on our place in the world and how to nurture and develop our state of happiness in a way that does not harm others. Does not "take" from others. Does not drain others.

That honors our self-interested nature, and yet, does not cross the line to selfishness.

But it only can be a reality if we each first take care of ourselves from within. By releasing the frustration and anger that accumulates. So we don't project it onto those around us. We don't "take it out on them." That is where self-interest crosses the line to selfishness. That's when we begin to hurt ourselves and others. Because if we are not "full" from within first, our tendency will be to look outside of ourselves for fuel sources, often other people. And our default is often to drain them so we feel better.

And the development of a life as a self-aware human being starts with self-recognition. So seeing that we sometimes cross that line is a critical first step. Then we can begin to do something about it. We can begin to change our behavior, catching ourselves more often when we see ourselves shifting to being selfish from our normal, innate state of self-interestedness.

But as I said, that cannot be done effectively by simply changing one's thoughts about this. It has to come from deep within. From the inner fabric of who we are. By stimulating that part of us that can release us from the binding influence of past stresses in our lives, and expanding our conscious capacity for mental experience that truly broadens our perspective.

Then we will feel inwardly more balanced and more naturally find ourselves living life from the normal, innate state of self-interest...with fewer wanderings into selfishness.

Giving & Taking

When my kids were very young, we taught them to "turn within" and take care of their own needs first. That was through being self-reflective, then making conscious choices in their lives, whether it was about themselves personally, their friends or other issues.

In the mid-1990's, while we were living on Rose Ave in Los Angeles, we had the idea to make it about choosing toys that they really liked — deciding which ones were meaningful to them — rather than just there to fill up the closet, to "collect more stuff."

When our son Jesse was 8 and his sister Sam was 2, we told them "no more toys!" until they chose which ones they wanted to keep and play with — because their closet shelves were piled up with toys that hadn't been touched in months.

Ever seen that happen, all you parents out there?

Of course, you have! I've been to some of your houses…

So we told them we'd have a yard sale and they could keep all the money from their toy sales. It taught them how to value what was important to them. And how to cull and filter both on a material and an internal "turning within" level.

Now, 24 years later, neither of them are collectors of stuff they don't need. They regularly donate extra clothes and other stuff to thrift stores and shelters…and my kids are not financially wealthy.

What does that approach do for you internally?

I think it frees us up to *give more*. Less energy is spent on amassing unnecessary material stuff, so we can use that energy to first "give" to ourselves, then give to others.

I also taught both kids my "Turning Within" Meditation

technique when they were 4 years old. This helps them "fill their tank" directly using their own mind to turn on that switch inside that "gives" to themselves first. So then they can later give more of "who they are" to others.

We often hear in our culture the phrase "it's important to *give back*." I'm a former very non-professional athlete and following sports teams is a passion of mine. So every Sunday, Monday and Thursday night now we hear story after story of an NFL player "*giving back* to his community..."

That's all good. I'm not knocking it. It's important for those who have much to help those who don't, assuming they want the help of course.

That said, I'd like to suggest a slight — but I think meaningful — change in how we might describe this when we teach our children.

I prefer to say "giving" or "being present" instead of "giving back." Being present to help others. Or simply — giving.

Because "giving back" implies either you have too much, which is a bad message. (Don't get me started on how much a pro athlete or entertainer makes compared to a schoolteacher....) Because no one should accrue too much stuff (money or possessions), much more than they really need, at the expense of others. Or, alternatively and equally reprehensible, "giving back" implies you're returning what you shouldn't have taken in the first place.

So I prefer "giving" or "being present." The NFL players were "present at their local food banks helping their community that was flooded by the hurricane...giving their time freely to help others in need."

Here is the point: "Giving" should always be without strings attached. Including without negative implications. Otherwise it's another form of "taking."

In a similar way, "volunteering to help others" when one is exhausted or sick, is yet another form of "taking," not giving. You are draining others of their life force when you're not "full" internally yourself. Okay, maybe we're never completely "topped off" full, but at least we need to be closer to full than to empty. And volunteering when your "tank is on empty" is not truly helping those in need. It certainly is not helping you who are in obvious need.

So again, I think we would do better as a society to each "fill our tanks" first — turn within and connect inside, whether that is through meditation, prayer or simply napping — before we turn our attention outwards to helping others. That's true giving.

What Is Thanksgiving?

As many of you know, I like to reflect, and I have memories, old memories.

So what's Thanksgiving NOT?

It's not the mythical celebration of the Pilgrims thanking the Native Indians at some "we're all One" dinner party with turkey and all the fixins'. The truth which our children should be taught is that when the local Indians helped the clueless Pilgrims survive their first winter, the Pilgrims later reciprocated by sending smallpox blankets to kill the Indians. Just like I remember the U.S. government doing again 200 years later to the Lakota (Sioux) and other Native tribes.

Yes. Genocide.

So that's not Thanksgiving.

Then what is it?

I think for many of us it is a time to reflect and thank those who are in our lives.

To thank them and "love" them in the way Jesus taught us. Jesus the teacher, not Jesus the religious idol. To love them and "accept them for who they are, not who we wish they would be." That's what he taught love is.

Now...accepting their strengths is easy. But what about their weaknesses?

That means we see their shortcomings. And we accept them — not by abiding or supporting their cruelties let's say, but instead — by seeing clearly those weaknesses yet, at the same time, not trying to change who that person is at their core. Because only they can do that. That's acceptance of that person. Loving that person.

And loving that person in that sense of "acceptance without trying to change" him does not mean we need to keep him or her in our close orbit. It could mean we separate and move away figuratively or literally. Yet that still constitutes "love" in the way Jesus taught.

These nuances of love have been lost over the past 2,000 years. Perhaps it's time we recalibrate our understanding of love so we can begin to "give" more fully. And be truly thankful in our gifts to each other of living life. Especially today...but every day.

Have a wonderful Thanksgiving!

Reincarnation And Living
In The Present

It's never easy to deal with your own death or the death of loved ones, even if you believe in reincarnation — past lives, future lives, coming back in another life in another body…

I talk about this in my lecture for those in the audience who believe in reincarnation, or who are curious about the possibility of its reality.

There always seems to be at least about 5% in the audience who believe in reincarnation — in a place like Malibu where I once gave a 4-hour seminar, there were as many as 30% in that belief category. So, yes, this belief is influenced by cultural and regional variations.

But, nevertheless, I always point out that even if we believe in reincarnation, there still is sadness because we are not seeing those departed loved ones now. Plus, even if we believe we will see them again later, we don't know how their personality might slightly change in a way that is significant to us, or if they might be a different age, gender, or change in who knows what other way that is different from how we know or knew them now…

All of that points to a major message of my "Overcoming the Fear of Death" lecture — *to live life fully now in the present*, not for after you think you're enlightened, or not for after you die and go to heaven, or not for after you get reincarnated, or whatever.

Living life in the present. It is key.

It has been the key message of almost every sage that has ever been — look at Jesus's messages more closely and you will see it there, look at his actions, his behavior — it is clear.

At Eternity's Gate

*starring Willem Dafoe as Vincent van Gogh
and Oscar Isaac as Paul Gauguin*

~ a viewer's reflection by Kelvin Chin

Many of you know my relationship with eternity. My intimate, personal relationship.

This movie reminds us of how Reality TV and the illusion of instant fame in the 21st century misleads us into thinking "what's important."

Instant fame

And I'm speaking especially to our world's Millennials and Gen Z's, many of whom are my most anxious and miserable clients — instant fame is not important. "Likes" and "Followers" can be monetized, yes it's true.

But in the grand scheme of things, it's not important.

Living and enjoying life in the present is what's important.

And "enjoying life" means at least *sometimes* doing "what you love to do." Okay, maybe you can't do what you love to do as your full-time employment — perhaps you're like van Gogh — due to its lack of popularity at the time and insufficient income potential, it is not feasible to support yourself. But you need to do it at least some of the time.

To feed your soul.

And who knows, maybe to feed the souls of others after you die. For eternity.

Maybe — like Vincent van Gogh — we are all living life at

Eternity's Gate.

So enjoy it now.

Hopefully with less pain and misunderstanding than van Gogh. But with as much passion and inner peace from your talent.

Paint the painting, design the invention, dance the dance, write the novel.

Not because you want to become rich and famous. But because *you love doing it.*

Let eternity take care of the fame.

Scary Dreams

Scary dreams can happen anytime of course — before or after we learn to meditate. They're not uncommon and happen when we're releasing old fears.

There are basically two kinds of dreams — fantasy dreams and creative dreams. Fantasy dreams can sometimes be fun and other times be scary. Creative dreams are the kind that we can get insights from.

"Turning Within" Meditation can facilitate both types of dreaming. Why? Because this meditation is waking the mind up to more of its creative potential, and at the same time is releasing old stress and balancing the system.

Plus, meditating in the morning right after waking up can also be helpful in spontaneously getting rid of the "cobwebs" sometimes left over from the scary dreams.

Whatever is causing the release, we don't know, but the meditation is definitely not causing the scary dreams — the stress that you have stored up for probably years (that you are often largely unaware of), is what's causing the scary dreams. Whether the meditation — or a combination of the meditation and your sleeping — is causing the release, we will never know for sure, but the releasing is what's good and important.

But regardless of what is causing the release, it's not uncommon to notice strong, powerful, and sometimes scary dreams. And the intensity of the emotional experience is always connected to the intensity of the stress that has been sitting around in the nervous system. So the more intense it is, the "better a sign" that you have released something very powerful that's been eating up a lot of your energy — psychically, emotionally, or physically — that you were likely not even aware of.

We live in a world, from a healthcare standpoint, which does not understand these things very well at all. We tend to live in a culture — and the healthcare world is part of that culture — where we think everything should be fine and smooth. And when we are free of symptoms, we incorrectly think that is when we are "healthy." ("Give me a pill, Doc, and make my problems/symptoms disappear!")

For example, just because you don't have a fever and sore throat does not mean that your immune system is strong. If you have been "burning the candle at both ends" staying up late and partying with little sleep after long days at work, you may have been gradually weakening your immune system, and the "symptoms" of sore throat have simply not manifested yet. The lack of symptoms does not mean you are healthy.

When the symptoms appear, they are just a sign of what is underneath, sometimes of tensions and imbalances lying deeply hidden beneath the surface — much like an iceberg — that have been accumulating sometimes for many years. Those are what are causing our problems and need to be released/balanced.

Also...

In the process of releasing, we often forget how many decades we've been building up junk in our system and while it won't take decades to get rid of that junk, the rebalancing process will undoubtedly have some ups and downs and not be a completely placid/even/flat situation. It's weird because we completely accept that we all sometimes have terrible times in our lives (and then when we get past them, we often forget that we went through the terrible times). However, when it comes to our mental/emotional/physical health, and when we're getting healthier, we somehow think (unrealistically) that we should be able to have no ups and downs...

The good news is that this simple meditation technique is accelerating the healing process exponentially because you are not only getting rid of old baggage, but also you are taking on less new junk.

The other thing that I tell people in my meditation classes is that our nervous system is also getting "used to" the balancing and releasing of old junk in the sense that our body does not know yet (especially if you just started the technique recently), that you are going to be doing it every single day twice a day. So the body jumps at the opportunity to try to get rid of as much baggage as possible as quickly as possible — which underscores the importance of the consistency and regularity of doing it twice a day in order to train the mind-body system that it can release the old stuff gradually...and does not have to try to release it all at once.

The body seeks balance, i.e., homeostasis.

The "Turning Within" Meditation technique allows the body and mind to naturally get what it has been seeking. In as easy and comfortable a way as possible.

Chapter 4

MEDITATION

How To Choose The Right Meditation Technique For You

When cultural icon Oprah Winfrey can't even decide which meditation technique is the "best in the world" to stick with, how can we mere mortals be expected to assess and choose — especially with so many different types of meditation in the marketplace?

Well, I'm going to give it a shot. At least I'll give you some key issues to look for.

I've been meditating for 50 years and have been exposed to many forms of meditation. Over the past four decades, I've taught thousands worldwide how to "turn within" and reduce their stress and anxieties, and increase their self-confidence and self-awareness through meditation. Many of them had tried other meditation techniques before finding me.

So, out of the hundreds of meditation techniques in the world, how do you know which one you should do? Here are some issues to consider.

GROUP OR INDEPENDENCE?

First, ask yourself: "Are you into groups, or do you prefer being more self-sufficient?" That is a threshold question to ask yourself because many encourage you to join their organization and meditate regularly with their group, or do it online with them, often through a subscription plan. Personally, I prefer to learn things that I can do on my own without having to schedule my life around other people's desires. But you may be different. Just ask and find out upfront.

DIFFICULT OR EASY?

The next question to ask yourself when choosing a meditation technique is "Do you prefer difficult or easy?" Most meditation techniques involve focus, control, concentration, or clearing the mind of thoughts. Those are guaranteed to be difficult. And often for most people, impossible.

A 10-year-old interrupted me in a lecture once and said, "Yeah, every time I try to clear my mind, I still have the thought that I'm not thinking any thoughts...which is a thought!" Brilliant. Message: Don't waste your time with that type of meditation. I'm into easy, and meditation can be effortless.

WAKING STATE METRICS

I'm often asked, "Why do so many meditation techniques involve focus or control?" I think it's because those meditation teachers do not have a full understanding of the mind, and haven't yet figured out that the mind operates differently in meditation than in waking state.

They've taken what I call "waking state metrics" and applied them to meditation. Of course that makes no sense because that would be like applying a dream state "yardstick" to waking state. So, if we were applying dreaming rules to being awake, we would then expect elephants to turn into flowers, or hallways to sometimes never end. But they don't. Because we know better than to mix yardsticks.

So why do so many meditation teachers mix them up in meditation, applying waking state rules to meditation? Simple: somewhere along the line they got confused.

REDEFINING "MEDITATION"

Thus the need for what I call the "Redefinition of Meditation." Whenever I teach meditation classes, a huge part of what I do is undo much of the confusion that many people have about meditation. The preconceived notions. The trappings.

In addition to incorrectly thinking that meditation involves clearing or focusing the mind, many think that it somehow has to be religious. Not so.

Many meditation techniques are rooted in religion. Buddhist, Hindu, Christian, and others. But there are meditation techniques that are not associated with religions. After learning Transcendental Meditation (TM) in 1970, studying personally with Maharishi Mahesh Yogi in 1971 and 1973, and teaching it for 10 years, I removed all religious and cultural trappings and made the process even easier and more flexible to fit into our busy lives. I now call the meditation I teach "Turning Within" or sometimes I just call it "learning how to let go."

I like to keep it simple.

Any meditation technique can and should be easy and effortless if the teacher knows how the mind operates and knows how to get the student "from point A to point B." That is a key issue to look out for when assessing the marketplace of meditation techniques. Most meditation teachers do a very good job at describing point B (where the student wants to get to), but few have the expertise to get the student from point A (where the student is starting from) to point B.

DIFFERENT TECHNIQUES, DIFFERENT RESULTS

We've all heard the basic health benefits of meditation — relaxation and stress reduction being the most commonly cited. However, are all meditation techniques the same in terms of results?

Not so, according to a number of scientific studies — several were compiled in a recent 2016 article, and there was a 2016 study published in *Psychological Science* indicating that Mindfulness meditation made meditators' memories less accurate. These are important studies because they show that not all meditation techniques produce desirable results.

In one 2013 study published in the journal *Brain, Structure and Function*, scientists showed that directing or focusing the mind does not have the same effect as a technique that allows the mind to experience what the researchers call "silence." Regular periods of silence seem to create new brain cells in the hippocampus, the part of the brain responsible for memory and learning.

I interpret their use of silence as "not directing the mind, not focusing it," because they contrast silence with techniques that focus the mind. Those focusing techniques do not create new brain cells. Interestingly, in a study published in the journal *Heart*, even listening to relaxing music — while it may feel relaxing — was measured to be not as relaxing as two minutes of silence. So, even listening to relaxing music seems to be experienced by the mind as "focus" and "directing the mind" and therefore less relaxing than not listening to anything.

DO OTHER TECHNIQUES INTERFERE — CAN YOU DO MORE THAN ONE?

We have discussed the differences among the many techniques, including the significant gap in results between techniques involving focusing and directing compared to an easy, effortless technique that allows more silence. But can you practice more than one technique?

Sure.

I have taught many students who continue to do other techniques afterwards. For example, I've instructed Buddhist monks to meditate. Of course, they meditate separately using their Buddhist meditation — that's what they do in the monastery all day. Yet what they say is that they get more out of their Buddhist meditations after learning mine since they say they feel mentally more relaxed and stronger afterwards. So, there is no conflict.

And I have taught clergy from all religions, including priests, nuns, rabbis, ministers, as well as Sikhs, Muslims, Hindus, and atheists. There is no conflict because I've removed all religious and cultural trappings from the meditation teaching and technique.

NOISY OR QUIET PLACE

You should be able to meditate anywhere. Literally. If your meditation teacher suggests that you should meditate in a certain place or under certain conditions — incense, candles, altars, no noise, certain background music — then just understand that they are speaking to you from a belief-based place, not a practical place. Those are trappings, i.e., stuff. Meditation involves your mind experiencing itself, albeit in a different way than it normally does when it's awake. But everything else is extraneous, not necessary. It's baggage.

So, whether you are in a noisy or a quiet place, you can meditate equally effectively. I've even taught meditation 30 feet down the hall from a rock band in a Recreation Center when I was teaching in the U.S. Army on the DMZ (Demilitarized Zone) in Korea. That was noisy! But the meditation worked regardless.

Meditation should be portable. You should be able to meditate as easily in noisy airport terminals, hotel lobbies, planes, trains, buses, and restaurants as you can at home.

FINAL THOUGHTS

While there are many different types of meditation techniques in the world to choose from, you need to pick one that works for you. That fits your lifestyle. That meets your life objectives and delivers the results you are looking for.

Don't just blindly follow your friends or family to the meditation teacher they chose. Ask questions first. Get answers to the types of questions raised in this article. Do this upfront.

Don't find out later that you joined a group that does not align with your values and how you expected meditation to be taught.

Be a wise consumer. It will serve you well in your life journey.

Why Bother To Meditate If You Don't Have Anxiety?

Hundreds of medical studies have shown us that meditation is perhaps the most effective way to reduce and eliminate anxiety. And we all know the many health benefits — both psychological and physiological — that can come from having less anxiety.

And there are legions of medical studies that demonstrate that meditation is also effective at mitigating or eliminating a wide range of physical health issues.

But why bother to meditate if you don't have anxiety or other physical health issues?

There are many reasons.

But first, let's ask ourselves…

THE REASON FOR LIVING

Why do we do anything in life?

I think the answer is quite simple — for our enjoyment, *to make us happy.*

Nothing more complicated than that.

But, it's huge, right?

So, what if meditation could make us happier so we could enjoy life more? Would that make it worth learning?

I suppose if your answer is, "No, I'm actually experiencing the maximum level of happiness I could ever experience in my life, so, nah, I don't need more happiness, I have enough of that!" — then, "Good on ya" as my Australian students would say. You are in great shape.

But most mere mortals would admit that there is always room for improvement — that we all could use a little (or a lot) more happiness in our lives.

So, here's how that happens through meditation…

OUR LIMITED VIEW OF OURSELVES

Most of us on the planet are walking around experiencing life through a very limited perspective, whether we know it or not, because we think (incorrectly) that our everyday mental experience is defined by "thoughts we have," and by "decisions we make." This is a very limited view of our mental experience — and thus our lives — because it means that our lives are just a series of thoughts and actions, a collection of all of that. And, what we tend to do is then think that we are *defined* by that.

That all of those thoughts and actions — that is *who we are*.

That is the fundamental mistake.

Because if that were true, then what happens when we have a different thought — and that happens about every split second sometimes, doesn't it?! Does that mean that our identity — who we are — is changing every split second? And if that were the case, how would that make you feel? Stable, happy? Maybe not so much, right?

Some people do believe that they are their thoughts and their actions. And those people tend to feel very unstable, "like a football being thrown around" by the whim of everybody else (their boss, their partner, their government, etc.) — they feel "out of control."

AN ALTERNATIVE VIEW OF OURSELVES

Instead, I suggest that there is something constant throughout all of our experience — and that is our mind. Our mind, our consciousness, our personality is what is constant.

We need it to even *have experience*. Our mind is *the experiencer* of our thoughts and actions. Not the other way around.

So, by defining ourselves as our minds, we can wrest control back to where it should be. Within each of us.

Instead of giving up control of our lives (and our happiness) to everything external to our minds.

THE MISSING LINK

But how does meditation fit in with all of that?

Meditation is that "missing link" in most people's lives. It allows the mind to experience itself outside of its limited "decision-making" mode. Because if we can allow our minds to expand outside of that mode, and experience its vastness — in a sense, "turning the lights on" in all the various dormant areas of our mind — then we become more self-confident, energized, and stable.

In short, we become more wide-awake and inwardly powerful. And we feel more in control, less like a football being tossed around on the "playing field of life."

We identify with what we really are. Our minds. But in this different, more expanded, less limited, more "free" way.

Through meditation, we can begin to experience directly the *structure* of our minds — its expansiveness and inner power. Not just the content of what's in our minds.

Would that increase your level of happiness?

You bet it would.

Learning Less In Meditation Teaches You More...

What?!

Does that even make sense?

How could "learning less" teach you *more* ? Let me explain what I mean by "learning less."

We live in a world where complicated solutions are praised and often worshiped more than the simple ones. Why is that?

I think that is because we tend to judge and assess value based on identifiable specifics. And the longer the list, the more we value that solution.

Let me be clear. I am a pragmatic, results-oriented guy. So yes, a list of beneficial results is absolutely a key measurement of any valuable solution.

But, what I'm talking about here is during meditation. And "during *meditation*" is not the same thing as "during *waking state*." Not being able to draw that distinction is perhaps *the* biggest mistake that most meditation teachers make.

Because it affects technique.

And when the meditation technique is "looking for specific results," then it involves focus and control. And focus and control is what makes meditation NOT work. Because as we said, the way the mind functions during meditation is different from the way it functions in waking state. Thus, we need to apply different rules in meditation from the rules we apply daily in waking state.

The most effective way to maximize benefits from meditation is to *not* look for specific results. To *not* focus, to *not* control, to *not* concentrate, to not try to clear the mind. This is the opposite of what most meditation teachers teach, and is the primary reason why most techniques are difficult and less than effective. They are applying waking state rules in meditation.

But what do you "do" in meditation? It can't just be sitting and allowing the mind to think, could it?

Again, do you see the root of the question? We are often asked through the "doing" lens, because we are used to "doing" things in waking state. The question is being asked from the wrong perspective.

The key to learning meditation properly is to find a teacher who understands how the mind operates differently in meditation compared to waking state. And who can teach you a technique consistent with that fundamental principle. Who knows how to apply meditation rules in meditation, not waking state rules. Who can show you how your mind can effortlessly transition from your waking state into your meditation state without focus, or control. A teacher who understands that meditation is *not* about having new experiences that you can add to your list of life experiences, but instead is about automatically turning on the "*opposite* of the Fight or Flight switch" and creating a situation where you can more deeply "know yourself" by allowing yourself to expand your conscious capacity for experience.

The key is not learning new content. It is learning how to expand the container of knowledge, our mind, our consciousness.

The Houston Astrodome Analogy

A visual image of how to address some of the age-old questions about the human mind...

About 40 years ago, I started using an analogy to describe "the mind" to people in a more visual way.

I had just instructed the senior executive team at a very large insurance company, whose regional office was based in Hong Kong. One of their executives had a PhD in psychology from the University of Houston, and when I was describing how much more of the human mind there is that could be experienced and unfolded through meditation, he interrupted and told us an analogy that his psychology professor often used.

I have been using it ever since...

THE ANALOGY

His professor told them to picture the then recently constructed Houston Astrodome (1965), which at that time was the world's first multipurpose domed sports stadium. It was huge for its time seating 75,000 in air-conditioned comfort. He said to imagine it empty — except for yourself sitting at the very top row of seats at the 50-yard line — and to imagine a small 8" tall bucket way down on the middle of the field with a dozen ping pong balls bouncing in and out of it. The professor said the Houston Astrodome was analogous to our mind, and that the bucket of ping pong balls represented the equivalent amount of activity going on in our mind, how much of the mind we each typically used.

Very little.

I have been using that analogy ever since to describe how much *more* of our minds we have to "wake up" and use. And that "turning within" through meditation is a way to wake up those dormant areas of the mind for us to activate, enliven, and use in our daily lives.

A VARIATION ON THE ANALOGY

Recently, I came up with a variation on that analogy to explain and help people understand an abstract principle of the human mind in a more concrete, visual way.

Inevitably in meditation, our minds wander. And if we are practicing a meditation technique like the one I teach — "Turning Within" Meditation — the mind will inevitably wander off of the technique, or off of the sound, and will be thinking all sorts of things. This is natural and normal in the meditation process.

When that happens, my students sometimes ask, "When I am meditating, and I get away from my sound, who is the 'I' that realizes that 'I' am not thinking the sound?"

The short answer is: *It is you, it is your mind.*

Your mind can have different perspectives, almost as if being in a different place — but that is not literally true — since it is still your mind, just from a different "viewpoint."

Here's the longer answer.

Most of the time, most of us are as if in the bucket. In other words, we are in and among the thoughts, activity, and focus of life — whether awake or meditating. But occasionally, during meditation our mind may automatically as if "step out" of the bucket and we can sometimes experience a different perspective.

But it is still ourselves having the experience of ourselves... just in a different way.

In those initially brief, fleeting moments like that, we experience ourselves "being aware we are not thinking the sound…." It is that momentary reflectiveness that is, nevertheless, "my mind" — just experiencing itself outside the bucket for a moment.

As we continue meditating over the months and years, the mind becomes more and more familiar with staying alert and conscious outside the bucket of activity. Yet, it still is "within itself" — it's still in the Houston Astrodome — it still is the mind experiencing itself, just in a different way.

You see, most of us don't have much conscious awareness of all the various permutations and nooks and crannies that exist in the vastness of our own minds. Many, in fact, have never really "stepped outside the bucket" to even realize that their minds are more than just what's happening in that bucket. Many have seldom experienced how much more interesting, expansive and *operationally* different in so many ways their minds can be, compared to what they are used to.

So, the experience of stepping outside the bucket is not only new for most of us…but also many of us haven't even experienced *that there is a bucket* — that our experience has been limited to the container we are used to being in.

FINAL THOUGHTS

I suggest that this whole notion of "the mind experiencing itself" is something we all need to experience in increments, in a "one step at a time" way. In a gradually increasing way…

And by taking those first steps of "turning within" and exploring more of who we are as individual minds, as we get to know ourselves better using this "from the inside out" approach, we quite naturally will expand the possibilities of our experience in daily life — giving rise to more creative, fun and effective lives.

Why Must Meditation Be Easy To Be Effective?

*This actually is a very simple question
with a very simple answer.*

First, let's agree on what meditation — regardless of which technique we're talking about — has as its objective.

Every meditation technique has this as its objective, although exactly how the teacher may articulate this may vary a little:

To turn on the Opposite of the "Fight or Flight" switch (i.e., the parasympathetic nervous system is the medical term) so we can reduce stress and anxiety, and expand our consciousness (i.e., our degree of wakefulness and self-awareness).

Second, let's agree that the "Fight or Flight" Response is an AUTOMATIC response in every human being worldwide. So to turn on the Opposite switch must be equally automatic.

This is why any effective meditation technique MUST be as automatic as possible — as EASY and EFFORTLESS as possible. You cannot turn on an "automatic" switch by trying to. Or by trying to control it.

It has to be ALLOWED to turn itself on.

That is the key element to an effective meditation technique. The more automatic, the faster it turns on the Opposite of the Fight or Flight switch. And therefore, the faster the benefits.

So, easy is a MUST.

Effortless is necessary for maximum benefits from meditation.

You simply cannot turn on an automatic switch by trying or focusing. It will not work, or it might work…but very, very slowly.

It must be easy and effortless. That's why my "Turning Within" Meditation is so effective and the benefits come so fast.

As I said, it's simple.

Why Do I Say That Meditation Should Be Effortless?

Meditation should be effortless if it follows the natural processes on which everybody's mind operates.

We all notice that our minds wander. This should therefore not be a problem that "needs to be overcome" in meditation. It should be embraced. If it is, then the meditation can be effortless.

Credit should be given to Maharishi Mahesh Yogi for bringing the world's attention to this fact — that meditation can and should be effortless. That it is the natural tendency of the mind to experience itself in this way — effortlessly — if you are taught properly how to set up the initial conditions to allow it. Maharishi was a spiritual revolutionary. He revolutionized the practice of meditation globally, and I predict he will be known by future historians of the 20th century for having shown us how it could be practiced effortlessly.

By inference then, any teacher of meditation who suggests or instructs that the student needs to focus the mind, needs to control it in order to meditate, or needs to clear the mind of thoughts does not yet understand the basic principles of the mind on which meditation operates.

This was Maharishi's gift to the world — his understanding of how the mind works. And it is a gift from him for which I am very thankful.

The meditation I teach is effortless. It is also more flexible and less complicated than the way I taught it in the 1970's. There are no rituals, religious trappings or lifestyle changes involved. Meditation should also be effortless in this way — it should easily fit into your daily life. It shouldn't have to take very long, and you should be able to do it anywhere. Alone or with others, quiet or noisy place, eating whatever you want, wearing whatever you wish.

Nothing outside of yourself should matter or affect the meditation benefits. It truly should and can be universally portable because you can take your mind anywhere. And it should be easy. If it is, the mind will settle down — easily and naturally — and experience itself.

Allowing The Monkey Mind To Be

Where does this commonly used term in meditation come from? The "monkey mind."

It comes from India. Where there are 50 million monkeys.

If you have ever traveled to India, one thing you will inevitably bump into, literally not figuratively, are monkeys. They are everywhere. In the cities, in the jungle, sitting outside your hotel, walking down the street sometimes right next to you. And if there are any trees around, you will of course see them not just sitting up in the trees, but going from tree to tree. And often looking for food.

So this expression comes from watching monkeys going from tree to tree, looking for the proverbial banana, all the time.

And so the idea is in order to keep the monkey from doing that, you need to chain it down. Prevent it from doing what it naturally wants to do. Control its behavior in that way.

In that culture, this principle which derives from the ancient Vedic tradition, has been used for millennia as the underlying principle of most meditation techniques. So in most ashrams — places where people learn meditation in India — that is the most prevalent teaching method.

But just because something has been around for thousands of years does not necessarily mean that it is a good thing. War has been around just as long. But using force to change other people's behavior, I would argue, is not a good thing for humanity even though it has certainly "been around a long time." In the same way, I do not think the subjugation of women for millennia has been a good thing for humanity even though it has also been around for a long time, and continues to this day.

You get my point.

So why don't we try a different approach? Back to our discussion about meditation approaches...

Instead of keeping the mind from doing what it naturally wants to do, how about allowing it to do the very thing that it wants to do...except in a slightly different way?

What is another principle of the mind that is also inherently active all the time, always going on in the background?

If you were sitting in a room studying some boring subject, or maybe even reading a nice enjoyable novel, and someone started playing your favorite song in the next apartment, what always happens? Your mind naturally wanders over to listening to that music. Doesn't it?

We all have experienced something like this not only many times in our lives, but I would venture to say: every single day of our lives, many times every day.

It's called "the natural tendency of the mind to go in the direction of more satisfaction."

Instead of making the mind do something it does not want to do, why don't we use that natural tendency of the mind and allow the mind to do what it wants to do anyway?

How do we do that? We give the mind something to think, but give it something that does not direct the mind in any particular direction.

Instead of being in fighting mode, we are in an allowing mode. And what does that do? That dissipates our resistance, melts away our tension, and allows the mind to relax and experience itself in this different way that we call meditation.

That is the underpinning of why an easy meditation technique can work so effortlessly. And moreover, I think more people would meditate if it was easier.

So teaching an easy, effortless process of meditation has been the way I've taught it for 47 years now. Just letting the monkey mind be — jumping from tree to tree — and overlaying my technique onto whatever the monkey wants to do.

Thus allowing him to settle down naturally
without force or control.
Effortlessly.

Effortlessness Redux

It's our birthright to know ourselves.
Knowing ourselves is inherent in being an immortal soul.
So, there should be no barriers to that,
including anything related to the meditation technique.

Let's talk about this idea of effortlessness in meditation a little bit more.

It is easy to say that meditation should be effortless. But what if you feel like it's impossible, that there is no way it could actually be effortless *for you*?

You might feel like, "Yeah, that makes sense. It is my birthright to know myself in this different way. But I know my mind. And there's no way I could ever get it to settle down." Have you ever thought that?

You might feel like you can't access your birthright, you may feel blocked. It's like you've inherited money, and it's sitting in a bank, but you feel like you don't have the key to the safe deposit box.

Meditation is the key.

Learning to meditate *effortlessly* "unlocks the door," unlocks this safe deposit box easily. And the key to meditating effortlessly is learning how to set up a situation where the mind is *conscious yet undirected*. If you learn how to set up those initial conditions properly, then the natural tendency of the mind will take over, and the mind will settle down. That is the key to learning meditation.

And after you learn this key, i.e., *the technique of how to allow that*, you can keep using the key, or you can "leave the door unlocked" for access anytime. Since it is your own mind, it's up to you!

In other words, you can continue practicing the technique as you were taught by your teacher, or…you may find that after some weeks or months of meditation that it becomes so *automatic* that whenever you close your eyes, your mind simply and effortlessly settles and experiences itself in this different way — the proverbial door has been unlocked, and access is easily granted whenever you choose.

Meditation can become that automatic.

When you first learn meditation, there is a technique that you follow. But, after you learn the technique, like all "techniques," it may eventually drop away.

I remember when I first learned to drive a stick shift, a manual transmission. I was helping some good friends move from Boston to Clinton, New York. We had a U-Haul truck and a manual transmission Toyota. At one point along the Massachusetts Turnpike, I was asked to drive the Toyota…but I had never driven a stick before. So, we took a slight detour to a large empty parking lot, and after some fits and starts, and lots of patience from my friends, I figured it out. Fortunately it was a straight highway with no hills! But, the point is that whenever I shifted for the next several weeks, I had to stop my conversation in midstream until I finished that stage of shifting — I could not talk and shift at the same time — because I was too engaged in "the technique" of shifting (coordinating both feet and both hands, etc.). But after that initial learning period, I could give a lecture if I wanted to while I was driving the manual transmission car!

The technique dropped away when I was comfortable with shifting while driving. It became automatic. This happens with all techniques.

And don't be surprised if this happens with your meditation technique as well. Eventually you can let it go — or, it may drop away all by itself.

Your mind will likely at some point become so used to experiencing itself in this different way during meditation (different from waking, dreaming, and sleeping) that the technique may fall away. And you will then become so easily connected with yourself every time you close your eyes to meditate that you simply — and literally effortlessly — experience your own mind in this way.

That is true effortlessness of meditation.

Redefining
"Purity Of The Teaching"

I have been meditating for 50 years, started when I was a teenager, have taught thousands worldwide to meditate for the past 47 years, led group meditations as large as 600 people, and have taught 25 meditation retreats.

There's a saying in teaching: "The teacher always learns more than the student."

With all that teaching experience has come the realization that meditation — and the teaching of meditation in particular — is not dependent on rules, ritual or dogma.

Most meditation teachers, regardless of which technique they teach, base their teaching on one or all of those elements. I think that emphasis is misplaced.

First let's look at the objective of meditation.

Why do we meditate? There are many reasons. But here are the overarching reasons:

- "Knowing oneself" (in the ancient Greek sense)
- Experiencing the mind in a different way than normal waking state (outside of the limited way we think of our minds — I call it the 8" plastic bucket we incorrectly limit ourselves to)
- Reducing stress and turning on the parasympathetic nervous system (the "opposite of the Fight or Flight response")

Here's the rub:

You can't turn on an automatic switch by control.

It is antithetical.

You can't allow the mind to experience itself outside the 8" plastic bucket by focusing it on being outside the bucket — that just keeps you *in* the 8" plastic bucket.

So effortlessness is key. No focus. No control. No concentration.

But is the teaching of a meditation technique that involves rules, ritual or dogma consistent with the idea of effortlessness? I think not.

It is "cognitively dissonant." That means it doesn't make logical sense. The theory and the practice don't match. It's like saying, "I'm a peaceful loving person." But then you do cruel and hurtful things. Your statement is inconsistent with your behavior. You don't "walk your talk." That's cognitive dissonance.

I would argue that if you inspect the teaching of even the meditation techniques that claim to be easy, that those teaching practices and techniques are not consistent with that objective.

Rules, ritual and dogma are three red flags of practices that are not walking the "effortlessness" talk.

Because if we're talking about the human mind, there is no ritual or dogma needed for it to "experience itself," even in the different way that we happen to be labeling and calling "meditation."

Let's discuss the "how" of meditation.

To be clear, I'm not suggesting a technique of simply closing your eyes and "Be." The "Be here now" or "Be in the present moment" approach is not a helpful technique for most people. Most people would say, "What the heck does that mean in practice?" Maybe it would work for a few, I'd estimate less than 1% could run with that minimal instruction.

Most of us need a bit more guidance and instruction. Perhaps even starting out with a technique.

So I am by no means against learning techniques. I am suggesting that "how" that technique is taught is crucial.

And that the teaching should also include the instruction that once the pathway to turning on the parasympathetic nervous system and expanding our conscious experience outside of that 8" bucket has been familiarized, the technique itself will often start to fall away.

It's like learning how to hit a ball with a baseball or a cricket bat. At first there's technique. Put your feet like this, hold the bat here, pull your arm and shoulder back this far, swing, etc. Then after you get the hang of it, you just hit the ball. The technique drops away.

It's no different with meditation. Eventually the mind just experiences itself in this different way and the body turns on the parasympathetic. Automatically.

But most of us need a technique first to get us from Point A to Point B.

So, back to the teaching of the technique and red flags for you to watch out for in selecting a good teacher.

Unfortunately most meditation teachers define "purity of the teaching" in terms of following the rules, ritual and dogma they were taught by their teacher. Following them exactly, following them without interpretation, following them "by the letter."

However, I've observed that that definition tends to create rigidity in those teachers, inflexibility and in some cases an authoritarian approach to the teaching. I think this is inconsistent with the whole concept of meditation in the first place.

Meditation should be about allowing the mind to experience itself in this different way as I said earlier. The key word is "allowing." But then you need a technique around that concept that is consistent with the idea of allowing.

And importantly, a teacher who is able to teach in a way that is consistent with that idea of allowing. That teacher needs to know where the boundaries are of course, where "right technique" and "wrong technique" reside. But within those boundaries, does that teacher give instructions and teach in a manner that is consistent with that "allowing approach"?

That is important because that will affect the teaching of the technique, and therefore the practice of the technique by that teacher's students.

So instead, I propose a re-definition of the concept of "purity of the teaching."

I think purity lies not in whether all of the teaching rules, ritual and dogma are followed verbatim, but whether the teacher teaches a technique in a way that is as easy and effortless as possible and has an attitude towards that teaching that is relaxed, easy-going, and open and receptive.

Because that attitude by the teacher will inevitably be perceived by the student, whether consciously or subconsciously, and is therefore an integral part of the teaching. Whether intended or unintended.

That is the reality.

So purity of the teaching primarily resides within the teacher him or herself. Their attitude. Their knowledge of the technique, of course. But their attitude supersedes even the rote teaching of their technique.

So as a meditator seeking a good meditation teacher, keep these principles in mind. And if you are a meditation teacher yourself, perhaps these principles will help you become an even more effective teacher of your students.

My hope is that sharing these principles, which are fundamental to the continued effective practice and teaching of meditation, will help ensure its continued longevity over the millennia to come.

Drive-Thru Meditation

"Turning Within" Meditation is NOT that.

We live in a culture that expects "a fix, a cure" immediately. We have no patience for waiting for a complete change. We are hungry now. We want the food, no matter how unhealthy, NOW.

The "now" of it is more important than the how it affects us long term.

Many people are the same with meditation. Are you?

Remember…

"Turning Within" Meditation is changing
"the structure of how you experience life."

(Read that again.)

That's not just getting rid of your symptoms. Your anxiety is merely a symptom.

Yes. I get it. No one likes being anxious. We want that feeling to go away. But what's *causing* it?

That's what "Turning Within" Meditation does. It helps you connect inside with yourself in a different way.

And that reduces 1) the intensity and 2) the frequency of the anxiety.

Over time. Gradually.

Not overnight.

Think about it. How long, how many years or decades have you been accumulating stress and anxiety? Does it make sense that it would disappear overnight?

"Turning Within" Meditation is not a magic pill. But

consistently practicing it will magically change the *structure of how you experience your life.*

How fast that happens is up to you and your nervous system.

Effortlessness &
Self-Acceptance

L et's look at the significance of effortlessness in the technique
and the development of self-acceptance within the individual
meditator.

As you have heard me say many times, effortlessness in
meditation can and should be a key component of any technique.
Here's another important reason why.

Effortlessness in the technique means that we are not
controlling, not manipulating the mind, or focusing it in any
way. We are allowing the mind to experience itself *in whatever
way it wants to experience itself* at that given moment in time.
We are not directing the mind, we are not making it go this way
or that way.

Our attitude is one of acceptance. And what are we accepting?

We are accepting *ourselves*. Our mind. Our mind at that
moment, *in whatever way it is thinking.*

And in that accepting, conscious yet undirected state, we
overlay the easy, effortless meditation technique.

So, the result is greater self-acceptance.

Contrast this with meditation processes that are not
effortless.

Those types of meditation techniques, for example, where
they instruct you to focus the mind on the breath, on a word,
phrase, a visual image, or look for some special experience or set
of experiences, or try to clear the mind of thoughts — those are
techniques of control, of subtle manipulation of the mind. And
they are difficult, because the mind wants to wander, to think
of other things. But those techniques typically do not allow

that natural wandering of the mind. And the mind finds that uncomfortable, and on a subtle level starts to reject it.

However, if that meditator continues to practice that type of technique over a long period of time, it can often result in a lack of self-acceptance. And this can eventually lead to a harshness, or an emotional "edge" expressed in that person's personality.

Instead, by practicing a meditation technique that promotes effortlessness, one ensures that one will promote one's self-acceptance of one's mind. And long-term, this promotes a resultant state of emotional acceptance, often expressed by a more nurturing, balanced, understanding quality to the meditator's personality.

Along with this emotional sensibility comes inner strength and self-confidence. So this self-acceptance does not mean a "softness" of the mind, emotions or personality — but instead, a personality that is sensitive to the needs of others (and to oneself), with an accompanying strong mind that comes from "knowing oneself" intimately, and easily, through effortless meditation.

Chapter 5

THE SPIRITUAL

We Are Not Disconnected From Each Other...

We are not disconnected from each other.
We are disconnected from ourselves.

The most common misstatement in the spiritual world — a world that has too often become an "echo chamber" of dissonant thinking — is that "We are all one."

The problem with that "external" focus on connecting *with others* instead of "turning within" and connecting *with ourselves* is that it continues the illusion and misguided belief that if we only can find more ways to connect outside of ourselves, then we will have world peace.

Peace on Earth.

More rallies, more town halls, more sit-downs to discuss our differences. Not true. We need to ask ourselves — what is our TRUE desire?

It is *inner peace*. Right?

Yet, ironically, by continually seeking it outside of ourselves, we push ourselves FURTHER away from fulfilling our true desire.

This "seeking peace by connecting with others" is yet another example of — once again — being fooled by our near-constant overemphasis on the "XYZ" side of the "Conscious of XYZ" model. That's the phrase I long ago borrowed from my good friend Charlie to illustrate our infatuation with the external over the internal.

If we don't each deal with our inner discord, then we will simply bring that discord to the rallies and town halls, and end up expressing that lack of inner peace in a myriad of externalized frustrations. We see it played out all the time.

And many spiritual seekers and their teachers are just as guilty of being seduced by the external. They may use less obvious terminology — they might not talk about "financial" materialism, for example, but materialism can be "spiritual" as well.

You might ask: "Who cares? Why does this matter?"

Because it causes people to stray further away from that "peace" that they so desire in the first place.

Focusing on the XYZ's lures us to be ever more distracted by trucks, flashy cars, big houses, clothes — and yes, even NDEs, STEs and other spiritual experiences that often elicit the "Wow, Gee whiz" reactions from those who have not had them. All of these are external in the way I'm defining it. They are all identifiable, concrete XYZ's.

External to what?

External to our *essential individual selves* — our minds. Each of our minds which are unique from each other.

That above sample of XYZ's are all simply experiences that someone may have. And experiences are fleeting — they come and go. So, "hitching your wagon" to fleeting experiences means by definition that your experience of happiness and peace will itself always be elusive — and fleeting.

And this leads to suffering. That's what unfulfilled desires cause — unhappiness. Lack of inner peace.

ONENESS OR "ONE-MESS"?

So, back to the idea of "connecting with all of humankind" as a means to happiness and world peace.

People think they are doing something wrong when they don't "feel connected" to all humankind. So they jump to the incorrect conclusion that the solution is to "experience that we are all one."

First, let's establish and agree that there is absolutely nothing wrong with seeking *connection* with others — as long as we first "turn within" to connect with ourselves before we seek happiness and peace outside. In fact, I think "connection" with others can be a source of great happiness in life.

However, "connection" is not the same thing as "oneness with all other beings." Connection does not mean "sameness." It does not mean "we merge" with all other beings.

This is a common misstatement in today's "pop spiritual culture."

So that we can travel as smoothly as possible along our respective paths to happiness, we need to be cognizant of the misplaced application of mathematical probability theories — like Quantum Mechanics — that have been contorted into allegedly "proving" this "oneness" theory.

Just because someone with a science background and an MD or PhD designation says it is so, does not make it accurate. Ask an actual expert in Quantum Mechanics if it is an accurate application of this theory. And also ask her if the theory was meant to explain physical reality. (Hint: it was not.)

Religious apologists abound on Earth — and on the Other Side. There is absolutely nothing wrong with being a religious apologist, but they should be honest and state that they are, that they — like religious preachers — have a belief that they are trying to persuade others to follow. Simply pointing to one's doctorate status and calling oneself a scientist while ignoring the consistent use of rational, logical thinking does not make the analysis "scientific."

The theory of oneness is a religious belief. Not a scientific fact.

Here's where it comes from…

Many thousands of years ago, a relatively small group

of, what we today would call, "spiritual leaders" each started having profound experiences of "connection" within themselves and extending outward — a feeling as if they were connected to all living and non-living things. This genuine experience was discussed over many lifetimes by these spiritual adepts and they quickly became a "self-referential" group, one where they started telling each other interpretations of that experience and then started postulating about what that experience meant in the larger scheme of things — in particular, human development. Thus was born the theory of "Enlightenment" — the idea that one might eventually develop to a point where one would "merge" with something they called "the Absolute" or "Oneness," a concept where the individual would lose his or her individuality.

The problem is that after 10,000 years of believing in this theory, not one of those spiritual leaders ever experienced the "merging" they had theorized about. So, they started rethinking the theory.

And now, they have relinquished that theory, and are convinced that the new theory of "life as a continual journey of making choices" makes more sense. Further, the making of choices (Free Will), they are pointing out, is something we each have control over. And they are encouraging us to make more consistent choices that align with bringing each of us more happiness.

So, even that early group of spiritual leaders who created the theory has decided to jettison the concept of "Oneness."

JESUS REMINDS US

What did Jesus mean when he said, "Seek the Kingdom of Heaven Within"?

He was reminding us to "turn within" — that is my 21st century translation of what I remember him saying. To him "prayer" was not asking for things. It was a simple yet profound means of "turning within" and connecting with oneself — that "Kingdom" of peace within each of us. Many of you do this daily — when you meditate, allowing your mind to experience itself, its essential nature within.

That is what he taught. He espoused "knowing oneself" in that internal way as a means to "bring Heaven on Earth." Translation: to uncover and draw out from inside of us that profound inner peace so that we can enjoy our lives here on Earth as much as we each can.

He was not saying to "deny" the external world. He was saying to enjoy it. To enjoy it with others. And to enjoy it maximally by "turning within" first.

BUDDHA REMINDS US

This is what Buddha meant when he said the world is an illusion.

He was advising us to "turn within" first. Not to be seduced by the wonder and beauty of the external world *at the expense of one's inner journey*. One's self-knowing.

He was not saying to divorce oneself from the world, as many have misinterpreted his words to mean. He meant just to go inside first. Connect with oneself — the true seat of happiness within. Not to merely get caught up in the external world.

That would be the path of illusion, according to him.

NOT NEW

So, these are not new ideas. They are ancient.

But I think it bears reminding from time to time through the millennia. Because for various reasons — primarily fear and desperation — I have seen us as a species get caught up and seduced sometimes by the purveyors of the "quick fix" who promise us salvation and "world peace" without each of us having to do anything on the inside.

Merely by dutifully following a belief system — whether it makes logical sense or not — an implicit or explicit promise of "perfection" is often made to us that never actually materializes.

My suggestion is instead to follow your own path. Do what makes sense to you. And connect with your own inner strength within.

Then you will bring a stronger sense of self — a more self-actualized, nuanced and powerful sense of your being — when and if you choose to connect with others and help bring greater harmony to the world we live in.

You are your best — and ultimately — only teacher.

Take yourself to class inside daily.

Attachment & Illusion

Where does the notion of "non-attachment" come from? It stems from the Vedic idea that we are not our thoughts and emotions. Those are our "experiences." Instead, the teaching point the Vedic teachers were trying to get across was that we are the "experiencer." Not the experiences. And that I think was their essential point. I agree with that distinction.

A point of identification I would also call it. That we should not identify our thoughts and actions with "who we are."

We are the experiencer. Not the experiences.

Make sense?

ILLUSION

Where does the notion of "illusion" come from in spirituality?

It stems from the Buddhist concept (Buddhism is an offshoot of the more ancient Vedic tradition) that the material world we see around us is also not "who we are" in our essence. So it is a similar concept to the previous one about "non-attachment."

So while I agree with those in principle, I caution us in following those ideas "in practice."

What do I mean by that?

What I mean is that the principles themselves as a description and suggestion of how we should view our waking state world are accurate and can be helpful.

But I do not think they were meant to be used as a *description of a technique or practice* of how to change our mindset, our perspectives, or conscious awareness about the material and non-material worlds, or the relationship between the experiencer and his/her experiences.

THE MISTAKE

Making that description into a technique, in essence, would be a violation, a misapplication of the following principle: "The description of where you want to go is not identical to the description of how to get there."

An obvious example to illustrate this point is working out in the gym. If you have a goal of doing 400-lb. squats, you don't go to the gym and immediately start doing 400-lb. squats. You start out with a lesser weight and gradually increase over time. Or, if you want to lose some body fat as a goal, you don't starve yourself by cutting out the equivalent weight of food. You get the idea.

While those examples demonstrate the point clearly, the following nevertheless seems to have been the most common mistake made in spirituality for millennia:

A description of the goal
has been taken to be the means for the path
to get there.

As I said above, the Vedic idea about non-attachment, and the Buddhist idea about illusion are both *accurate* descriptions of reality, that the material world is not all that exists. And that we should not get attached to our thoughts, desires and emotions since they are not who we are — we are our own unique individual minds which are experiencing those experiences.

However, how those ideas are put into a self-development practice is where the "rubber meets the road." Because that inner practice determines all-important outcomes and effects in our daily lives.

Understanding that our minds are distinct from — and not the same as — our thoughts and emotions is an important knowledge point.

That said, using the notion of "non-attachment" as a meditation *technique*, where one tries to remain "unattached" from one's thoughts and emotions is an unnecessary and ill-advised jump that often has unintended negative consequences. In my meditation teaching, I would describe that as a *forcing* of the mind which the mind resists and then contracts from. This is the exact opposite of what a meditation technique is meant to promote.

Similarly, seeing the material world as "illusion" and using that as an inner mental practice can lead to a dislike — even a contempt and divorcing of oneself from the world. Long-term practice of such techniques can also lead to halting speech, indicating a lack of full integration of thought and emotion into the speech pattern and behavior.

Why does this happen?

Separation and control. By continually manipulating or forcing the mind into that state, a sort of "split" can occur.

Consistent practice leads to greater separation — separation of mind, body and spirit. Again, the exact opposite intent of meditation techniques.

A REDEFINITION

Instead, an effortless technique of allowing the mind to experience itself in a natural uncontrolled, non-manipulative way nurtures a growing state of connection within oneself. Integration. Coordination and balance among mind, body and spirit.

The goal or objective of any meditation technique should be the same. Allowing the mind to experience itself in this different way is not the same as applying the experiential rules that we apply in waking state. Instead, applying "meditation rules" in meditation leads us to "allowing our mind to experience itself" in this different way that we label and call "meditation."

That's it. Nothing more complicated than that. But the key is how you get there. The practice itself.

So in the end, technique is everything. But once the pathway is established, and very familiar, even the technique will eventually drop away.

Those meditation teachers who understand and apply these basic principles are the ones who understand more fully how differently the mind operates in meditation than in any other state. Those are the teachers who can help you accelerate your self-knowing, your unique personal growth.

Can We Manifest Things In Our Life?

There are many spiritual teachers who conduct workshops with titles like this.

What's the truth about it?

Because it sounds magical, doesn't it? It conjures up visions from movies like the Avengers and other Marvel comic book or video game characters, or for those of you who are older — TV cartoons and Disney movies with sorcerers teaching their apprentices the trade...remember the wild, crazy broom scene?

Of course — that's exactly the "Wow, Gee whiz" reaction they want you to have. Why? Because then you'll listen, maybe even fork over the $5,000 or $50,000 for the seminar or conference to buy the "magic formula" that manifests anything and everything you want without actually having to do anything. Isn't that the magic pill everyone always talks about?

Let's discuss reality here.

The reality is that of course we manifest everything in our lives. We each are independent, sovereign minds. And we each have Free Will, personal choice to do what we want. So who else is manifesting our lives? Some panel of beings on the Other Side?

No. There is no one else involved.

We are always creating our lives. Every moment. In the continual present. By every thought we have and every action we decide to take.

So where and why does this seemingly mystical notion of "pure manifestation" come from?

I think one source of this confusion could be the experiences we have in our dreams every night. Are we "creating" what is happening in our dreams? Yes, our mind is creating those visions and experiences. However, are you actually flying when you are dreaming that you are flying? Of course not. You are just having a fantasy about flying, and yes, it feels wonderful and freeing, and all of that — so it "feels" real. And in a sense it is — it is a real dream experience. But not an experience that is transferable to waking state — just ask Icarus (the Greek guy who tried to fly with waxed wings too close to the sun).

Now you may wonder — what about those unusual dreams where you may have some intuitive, psychic type experience, not the usual fantasy experience I described above? Yes, that can happen in our dreams too. However, those are not us "manifesting" what we "see" in the experience. That is our mind psychically connecting with another mind and "reading" what they are thinking. Or, in the case of our getting an intuitive "insight" into what seems to be a future experience, that can happen because, again, our mind "tunes in" and can see the probabilities of something happening, and get an inkling about that upcoming event. But, those are not examples of "manifesting something out of nothing."

I realize that most people have not had those types of psychic experiences, so let me give you another example that is more common to all of us. Perhaps the following might offer another, more everyday explanation for where and why this mystical notion of "pure manifestation" comes from.

Think about it this way.

Let's say you came to a planet of people, or even on our own planet to a culture of people who had never seen the making of manmade fire before. Suppose you hit two stones together right in front of this culture of people, and a spark was created and you started a fire, you would be considered a sorcerer, a magician, a "god" — someone who could do the impossible. Someone who could "manifest" fire out of nothing.

But you and I come from cultures that know about flint, a certain type of stone that, if hit a certain way by another object (iron pyrite or steel), will cause a spark, which when it touches certain flammable objects (tinder), will ignite them. Thus the fire will start. We understand that technology, and the science behind it. So we don't consider it magic. We don't consider it "pure manifestation" out of nothingness.

It's normal for us.

Let's apply that example to the question at hand.

Are there people today who do not understand how the mind works? Who do not understand that thinking is the basis for action? People who just get totally caught up in the "doing" of life, going from task to task, without much forethought of how they get from here to there?

Yes. There are such people. However, I think most of us *understand* those basic principles. That it is not magic. That this is simply the "technology" of the relationship between our thoughts and actions. First come the thoughts, then the actions.

Let's take it another step.

Most of us understand that if we strengthen our thinking, we can make clearer decisions, and therefore our actions will be more effective in meeting our goals and objectives. Right?

I think most of us understand that this is also not magic. We are not manifesting something out of nothing by waving some magic wand, or thinking some magic words, or lighting some magic candle, or burning some magic incense.

We are simply taking a different approach — not merely changing WHAT our thoughts are, but seeking to change HOW we are thinking the thoughts, the power behind the thoughts themselves.

Assuming this is obvious to you, you have probably tried to strengthen your thinking, but whatever you have tried has not been sufficient. The seminars so far have not yielded the promised results.

The key is How.

How can we strengthen our minds — access the true vastness of our minds — so that our thoughts are significantly more powerful? What we have attempted so far has not been game-changing.

We want game-changing. That is what "magical" really means — something that we haven't seen before, an approach that is not widely taken. Just like banging two stones together to make a fire.

So what is the "how"?

The key is finding a way that is not simply "content-oriented" — not just learning more information — but instead how to *expand* our abilities. By effortlessly "turning within," we can experience the power of our own minds, connect with ourselves deep within, access that internal power that we all have, and then we can express it and actualize it through our thoughts and actions. That is the most powerful, direct approach to manifesting what we want in our lives.

Not by waving a magic wand, or reciting some incantation, but by first strengthening our connection within — "between me and myself."

That's how we can manifest our lives in a productive, effective, more joyful way with less stress and tension, and more ease and success. Not through magic, but through what we already possess — the vastness of our own minds.

10 Spiritual Red Flags

1. Scientists or spiritual teachers who espouse the Laws of Thermodynamics, especially the First Law ("energy cannot be created or destroyed"), who also talk about God or anything being the "Creator" of the Universe. There is no need for such a creator if energy cannot be created or destroyed.

2. Spiritual teachers who speak about Eternity and the Creation of the Universe. It is impossible. They are mutually exclusive. Either the Universe is eternal, i.e., beyond the measurement of time, uninfluenced by the field of change, or it's not. If it's eternal, that means — with no beginning and no end. Creation requires a beginning.

3. Spiritual teachers who tell you they are not your gurus, but expect you to follow what they say without question because they "know what is good for you." If it walks like a duck, talks like a duck, it's a duck. Or guru. Look at their actions, not just their words.

4. Ditto #3 for angels or other spiritual teachers channeling from "the Other Side."

5. Spiritual teachers who tell you that you are being or will be judged spiritually by anyone, now or after death.

6. Spiritual teachers who tell you that you are being or will be punished spiritually by anyone or that you get "credits" for doing good deeds (Hell, karma, etc.).

7. Anyone who tells you they know your "level of spiritual development," your "level of consciousness."

8. Spiritual teachers who say there is an end point, a goal, a state of perfection, e.g., Enlightenment, Nirvana, etc.

9. Anyone who uses "Destiny" or phrases like "It's meant to be" to describe a pre-ordained result or pre-determined path that is absolutely certain. Because this violates the principle of Free Will — choice.

10. Anyone who uses the existence of the Afterlife or other lifetimes (reincarnation) as evidence that God exists. They are two very different concepts. We can have experiences and memories of both "Heaven" and other lifetimes — and still be an agnostic or atheist, i.e., a non-believer in God. The Afterlife is a structural place that exists whether you believe in God or not.

Virtue

With the recent college admissions scandal dominating the 24/7 news cycle in the U.S., I was reminded once again about the idea of "virtue" that has been contemplated and preached about for millennia.

At first blush, one might think that virtue was totally lost in the minds (and hearts) of those (so far) 50 defendants indicted on March 12, 2019 in this $25 million (so far) scheme to gain access to elite colleges in the U.S. And from a certain point of view, I would have to agree with you. However, I think there is another perspective at play here.

A more insidious one that we as a culture should be aware of. Because self-awareness is the first step to change. And recognizing the need for change is the next step in doing something about it. Perhaps even doing something that is more aligned with one's inner desires that may, at the same time, actually result in less harm to others — simply put, a more enlightened approach.

VIRTUE

What do most of us think when we think of the idea of virtue?

I think we think "doing what's right," "following the rules of the game," "being a good person." Things along those lines. Right?

I think that is a fair definition — at least that is the way we generally have thought of virtue in the past 2,000 years. In the times of Jesus, the idea of "sin" was really meant to be "not following the Jewish rules," or "not following or obeying the rules of God, the Ten Commandments," etc.

However, about 500 years earlier, around 2,500 years ago in ancient Greece, the idea of virtue meant something deeper, more intimate. It included the idea of "self-knowledge," knowing oneself — so it was a more inward way of looking at the concept of virtue. I would argue that it was a more *practical* way of discussing virtue.

Because rather than arguing over whose rules about the world were right and wrong — and how closely you followed them — to determine whether you were a "virtuous person" or not, the Greeks in 500 B.C. instead looked within. They "turned within" and asked each person to candidly ask themselves what they found. Did they like what they saw? Did they see anything that needed change? Did they do anything about changing it? Did they "love" what they saw? Did they embrace "who they were" from the inside out?

It was an approach of valuation that was "self-knowledge" focused. Internally focused. Not externally focused.

And yes, while it was most certainly subjective, it did cause people to pause, reflect, go inside, and be introspective. I think there was something healthy about that process that the wider Greek culture benefited from.

Fast forward to today, 21st century planet Earth, and specifically 2019 U.S. culture.

MATERIAL WEALTH

Today, I think we find ourselves valuing money and wealth accumulation above all else.

We used to value innovation and education more so, and wealth was sometimes a side effect of those pursuits. However, I think in the past 50-60 years or so — starting in the late 1960's — especially when executive compensation started becoming more tied to stock prices because their compensation was more and more based on the liquidation of their stock options, we have gradually moved more towards valuing money and the accumulation of wealth above all else.

We now equate "who we are" — our personal identity — with our money and accumulated wealth — whether it is real wealth or just "perceived" wealth. We value ourselves based on money.

A few in our culture have "real" accumulated wealth — hedge fund managers, professional athletes, "A-list" TV and movie stars, CEO's of Fortune 1000 companies, a handful of big law firm partners, and former U.S. Presidents. But most of us are not that. Most of us just have "perceived" accumulated wealth — driving a Mercedes on a 3-year lease, living in a 5,000 square foot house with a $10,000 a month 30-year mortgage, or maybe living in a 400 square foot studio apartment but carrying a $3,000 designer handbag. That is perceived accumulated wealth. Not real.

But it represents the aspirations of our culture. It represents the values of our culture. To be "seen" as wealthy because "accumulated wealth" means "respect." It means "I am somebody" in our current U.S. culture.

"I am important."

At any cost.

And "at any cost" means we have become a culture of "the ends justify the means."

Anything goes. Even paying people to take your child's college entrance exam, or photoshopping her pics to send to the universities feigning your child's ability (and even her interest) to be on the coveted school athletic teams! And I bet that many more than 50 parents are guilty of having done so — I would guess the number is much closer to 100,000 nationwide. Not all wealthy like the celebrities, hedge fund CEO's and law firm partners in the current criminal lawsuit. But many more parents from the next socioeconomic tier down. That is my guess.

Because it is a reflection of the values of our 2019 culture. Money has become the metric to measure the "value of a human being." Not their wisdom, moral compass, kindness, or their ability to bring happiness to others.

A NEW "VIRTUE" GOING FORWARD

Yes, even in ancient Greek times, money and wealth accumulation existed. There definitely was an aristocracy — the wealthy and the working class, and even slaves. But virtue was understood in terms of "looking inside," and so each Greek, regardless of social or economic status, was highly valued as an integral part of the culture during much of that period.

Even 400 years later, the Roman emperor Marcus Aurelius — who was an avid student of Greek history and philosophy and fluent in Greek himself — eschewed his aristocratic birth and in his youth chose to sleep on the floor as was the habit of Stoic philosophers. "Turning within" was an integral part of his life, not just as a child but throughout his adult life.

I think today we need to get a grip on who we are as a culture, and as human beings as a whole. Because we have lost touch with who we are. We have externalized "who we are" and "how we value ourselves" so much so, that the college admissions scandal we are mesmerized by now is simply a symptom of a deeper disconnect.

A disconnect within. Within each of us.

We are who we are on the inside — regardless of color, wealth, nationality.

We are not our $650 per month Mercedes sedan. We are not defined by which elite university our kids graduated from.

We are defined by who we are inside, which determines the types of actions and behavior we execute on the outside.

And to make those types of choices more in alignment with

our desires that are less likely to hurt others, we need to "turn within" and develop ourselves from the inside out. That is the "virtuous" path that feeds us, that nurtures our souls, and that helps others in their quest for happiness.

A new — yet ancient — definition of "virtue" going forward is what is needed.

Spiritual Materialism
Revisited

What is "spiritual materialism"?

It's when we use materialistic metrics to measure our degree of spirituality.

I think most of us are familiar with the idea of "materialism" being used in the financial context. "Oh, he's so materialistic, all he cares about is how much money he makes!"

That sort of refrain. We've all heard it.

I'm suggesting that we could also apply the idea to spirituality.

First, those of you who have been to spiritual workshops, read books, or seen YouTube videos have undoubtedly witnessed people describing so-called "spiritual experiences" of various kinds. Whether it's feeling peaceful in meditation, visions of past lives, NDE's, contact with dead loved ones, or just feeling connected with all things.

To name a few.

The range is wide and the variation is vast. The point is getting caught up in any one of them is a form of "materialism" that may be self-limiting. Here's what I mean…

Sure. The experience may feel good. And it may be a wonderful experience. But does it define who you are? That's what I mean by "self-limiting."

Aren't you more than an experience, or set of experiences?

Instead, I see ourselves as different experiencers who — each in the uniqueness of our individualities — can experience the ever-changing vast universe in which we live in a myriad of ways. Not limited to one experience or set of experiences. No matter how supposedly "spiritual" in nature.

Food for thought.

Another way I think about "spiritual materialism" involves money itself.

I have seen over the millennia many seekers define their spirituality in terms of "not pursuing" or "not being seen as pursuing" financial gain or displaying having money. "Having no material possessions" or "having a disdain for the material aspects of life."

I saw it in the 1970's and I see it now. And I saw it 2,000 years ago. It is an ancient belief cultivated by religions for millennia. The "austerity" path. The path of the monk or nun.

There are even extreme examples 1500 years ago of Christian ascetics in the Middle East, supposedly "the holiest of holy men," each living on a small 3' x 3' platform at the top of a 40-50 foot pillar for up to 40 years, never coming down. Their spiritual disciples would climb up ladders to feed them, and since they never bathed (thinking it was not "spiritual" to do so), the disciples had to wear bags of scented herbs and oils to breathe through due to the horrific smell of their spiritual masters.

This also is a form of spiritual materialism. It is a self-limiting way of defining oneself as "spiritual."

I have been guilty of it in my past (okay, not the washing avoidance, or sitting on the pillar...). But, none of us are immune. This misplaced belief of "giving up" material things to demonstrate our spirituality is deep and engrained in many of us. And it can sometimes follow us around from lifetime to lifetime embedded in our emotional patterns, hidden below the surface level of our minds.

For example...

Whether you own 10 pairs of shoes or 100 pairs does not define your degree of spirituality. Whether your child goes to Harvard-Westlake or Mar Vista Elementary also does not define your spirituality.

Those are material choices that we each make based on our personal likes and dislikes and our individual needs, combined with our financial means. Maybe you're a dancer or an athlete who needs many pairs of shoes, or maybe you just like different styles of shoes!

Either way, it's fine. Your shoes do not define "who you are."

Maybe we choose the private school because the public school is overcrowded, and either we can afford the private tuition or we get a scholarship. However, the mere fact that our child goes here or there does not define our degree of spiritual strength or our "commitment to a spiritual life."

Maybe we need to cull how many shoes we have for stylistic change or simple wear 'n tear reasons, that's fine — but the mere number does not define us spiritually. We can own 500 pairs and be very committed to our inner spiritual sense of self. And conversely we can own 2 pairs and be utterly forgetful of our self-love and self-care.

I have a friend who owns so many shoes she has a separate bedroom to store them in! And she hires someone to switch the seasonal shoes every 6 months. Okay. Maybe that's a little bit extreme. But she's a very spiritual person on the inside.

Conversely, I have an old friend from 2,000 years ago who today still harbors this "lacking of material things" belief about himself and his spirituality. He has struggled his whole life — and for many lifetimes — with the self-limiting effects of this belief on his daily life, thinking "this is the way to be spiritual."

I used to naively think that sleeping on the floor like other Stoic philosophers was being spiritual. My mother quickly disabused me of that behavior back in the 2nd century. But to be honest, it took a while longer for my beliefs to completely change. Several lifetimes even.

And there's nothing "non-spiritual" about driving a Mercedes. But realize that it's just a car, no more or less spiritual than driving a Honda.

Spirituality is internal. Not external. The material external world is beautiful and should be appreciated. The cars, the shoes, the schools. But they are not who we are.

Similarly, as I mentioned earlier, we are not "spiritual" as measured by how many self-development workshops we've attended. There is nothing wrong with taking classes to enrich and expand one's understanding about life and the universe. However, the cautionary note is to watch out for replacing the "turning within" process with more and more content knowledge.

The consistency of "turning within" continually "expands our conscious capacity for experience," the container of knowledge. That is the key — typically for most people the missing key — to true self-development.

Simply immersing oneself into yet another spiritual workshop could be yet another expression of spiritual materialism. Adding more content to an already full container. Yet another way to distract ourselves from instead establishing a firm foundation with the basis of spirituality — our expanded sense of self.

Maharishi Mahesh Yogi, one of my teachers this lifetime, used to tell us his "Capture the Fort" analogy. I have modified his analogy slightly by replacing his idea of pure consciousness with my idea of the vastness of our individual consciousness. (Because as you will see in other essays I have questioned the validity of the idea of "pure absolute" consciousness.) Instead, that's what I now simply refer to as "our mind," who we are.

But his point is still applicable. Namely that we need to "capture the fort" — directly experience and establish regularly a firm connection with our inner self. What I now view as our vast eternal individuality.

And not get caught up in developing isolated skills — e.g., mind reading, astral traveling, and other esoteric and sometimes flashy experience-based distractions. Not even, as I teach in my "Turning Within" Meditation classes, getting caught up in any one experience DURING meditation that may be more pleasant than the next.

That also is yet another subtle form of spiritual materialism.

I came up with another analogy last year that explains this...

Picture your mind as a 100 million room castle. With most of the lights off.

However, realize that most humans are born — live their entire 70, 80 or 90 year lives and then die — having lived in just 3-5 rooms.

Imagine if you could "turn within" and allow the conscious mind to explore the rest of those rooms in the castle — which is your mind. Simply by effortlessly "letting go" of the focusing part of your mind, and letting the mind "explore itself."

By doing so, it automatically lights up the previously unlit rooms in the "castle" to reveal the vastness of ourselves to ourselves. Since they were previously not lit, you didn't even know they existed. But now, since you have turned the lights on in more and more of the rooms, you increasingly realize the vastness of who you are. You now have "actualized" the potential of your mind that has always existed, yet has remained untapped and hidden.

That is what I suggest true self-development is based upon.

And to continue with the castle analogy...

We need to be aware not to get stuck in any of those individual rooms — e.g., the calmness and extreme silence room, or the room that is full of light, or the room that makes us feel connected to all things, or the intuition room, etc. Because all of those are simply more experiences — and all experiences are fleeting. They come and go.

Instead, keep allowing the mind to expand its capacity. Lighting up more and more rooms in the castle.

Because that encourages our continued growth. Not in a content-oriented way. Not merely by learning more material or by learning a new "mental trick" or technique.

But by expanding our conscious ability to directly experience more of who we are.

For me, this has been the key to continued self-realization. To continued opening of myself to myself. With little or no distraction from the seduction of spiritual materialism.

Spiritual Insecurity

This is an affliction that is worldwide. It goes beyond borders and cultures. It is reflected both in our language and in our behavior.

How many times have you heard people say the phrase, "It was meant to be...," or "It must have been our Destiny..."? And yet afterwards, still say they feel on shaky ground.

Look at our behavior — at how disciplined some people are about attending spiritual services at their respective institutions. How many stories have we heard about people who have "never missed a daily or weekly service," or "never missed a meditation in their lives" — even if it meant keeping their friends waiting for hours while they finished their 2-hour program? What drives them to allow their spiritual practice to be so controlling of their lives?

I think it may be an underlying fear, and *insecurity*.

And perhaps in the case of "Destiny," that if we cannot predict everything, then we must at least make up something (that we cannot logically explain) and throw it under the catch-all concept of "it was meant to be." Otherwise, we feel like we are "out of control." And that makes us feel very uncomfortable at our core.

Or, maybe we feel the need to attend every spiritual service or meditation session without fail, because then we will feel that we have done everything possible to align ourselves with the "unseen powers" — people will use terms like the Universe, the Source, the Oneness, the gods, the angels — whom we believe are smarter or more powerful than we are, and whom we believe are somehow in control of our lives.

This spiritual insecurity is also reflected in our thinking.

We think of ourselves as small, weak, and unenlightened beings in the universe. And we think somewhere "on the other side of the veil" there are omniscient (all-knowing) beings or at least beings who are smarter than we are, and that we need to listen to them — unquestioningly — if they give us guidance.

After all, they are so much smarter than we are, aren't they?

First of all, I don't think that's necessarily true.

Making generalizations about the intelligence or wisdom of a mind *merely* based on whether it has a body attached to it (or not) could be disastrous. *Bottom line:* some minds are wise and some are not. Therefore, some you listen to and some you don't.

I think some minds who are on the Other Side, *may* sometimes be smarter and wiser than we are. But, *merely* because they are on the other side of the veil *does not* make them automatically smarter. It just means they do not have to eat to feed a biological body!

There is less difference between this side and the other side in that respect — *a mind is a mind* regardless of which side it's on, *regardless* of whether it has a biological body attached to it or not. Plus, consider this: does it make sense to follow someone's advice here on Earth about your sex life or your dietary nutritional needs, if that person has never had sex or had to eat food? No. Then why would you blindly follow that advice from a disincarnate being who has only lived on the Other Side and has no experience living on Earth in a biological body?

Some people who have had NDE's (Near-Death Experiences) point to the experience of having a more expanded mind, a mind that seems like it could "travel anywhere." They point to that as a difference between this side and the Other Side. In fact, that may be a source for this conflated belief that minds on the other side are inherently smarter and wiser.

And that sense of "expanded mind" on the other side may very well be a significant difference between this side and the Other Side — especially for many people who have not had sufficient experience of "turning within" while they are still in physical form on this side.

However, by allowing one's mind to regularly experience the "turning within" process, and by experiencing the natural and almost fluid expansion of the mind as it experiences itself in many different ways during that process (as I have described in my essay on the Houston Astrodome), each person can develop a familiarity with that more expanded mental experience — much like what people describe when they have Near-Death Experiences.

By developing that level of familiarity with one's own mind, one becomes more grounded *within oneself*. And that creates a natural state of self-knowledge and experience on which one's beliefs about reality can be more firmly built.

This would be a way to develop a stronger sense of spiritual security — from within oneself — starting by first simply turning within and developing a greater knowledge of oneself in the ancient Greek sense.

And from a practical standpoint, it's this type of spiritual security that we each can develop within ourselves now on a daily basis — enjoying it on a moment to moment basis — while living our lives here on Earth. And then not only will this sense of spiritual security help us in enjoying our lives while we are in our bodies, but also since it's within us — within our minds in which this security exists — we will carry it with us while we make the transition to the other side of the veil and while we experience life over there as well.

Spiritual Teachings That Create Suffering

What red flags should you watch out for
when choosing a spiritual teacher?

I think what is most significant is if a teacher is teaching something that in any way promotes an alleged understanding — what I would call a "belief" — in some other stage of life where the experience is supposedly fuller, better, or greater than living now in the present — whether that is a promise of some higher state of consciousness, or a promise of heaven, nirvana, enlightenment, or of living life in some other dimension.

If I hear that, or something resembling that, then that's always a "red flag" to me to question the depth of understanding, and even perhaps the motivation of that teacher.

Because all that really matters in life is living *in the continual present*. Because all we really have is the present. Everything else is imagination. The past has already happened, and the future has yet to occur — and given that Free Will is always in play, the future is always subject to change.

And living life in an imaginary world, in a fantasy world, is the opposite of *living life*. It is the opposite of reality. It would be the ultimate in teaching a student to live his or her life in some projected reality, in living in a fantasy world.

Many spiritual teachers unfortunately promote this type of thinking — maybe unwittingly, but nevertheless they do. They may do it for their own selfish reasons, or they may do it because they honestly think it's the best path for their students. And that belief by the teacher is usually based on *their* having blindly followed *their* teacher themselves, without having really synthesized and integrated the teaching within their own minds — without having questioned those mental constructs and without having developed their own unique version of that structure of thought.

Many times that happens because the tenets of the tradition they come from actually explicitly state that either "unquestioning devotion" — or sometimes what is referred to in Vedic or Indian culture as "Bhakti" — is a foundational precept on which the teaching and learning must take place.

That is also another huge red flag. It is a powerful precept because by definition it is based on the heart, on the emotional draw between the student and teacher. And that is hard to shake. It is difficult for the student to rationally see clearly beyond that cloud of emotion. Plus, as I mentioned, they are often encouraged and maybe even told "not to question."

But I think it's crucial to realize that this type of thinking where it's focused on our *prospective* life "in the future" — that postponing one's happiness until some goal is reached or some state of being is attained — is *harmful* and actually *contributes to suffering*.

It contributes to suffering because it discourages or disallows the individual from enjoying the moment, enjoying the now, enjoying their *current* experience. There is always something better, always something that the person feels they should be experiencing that is "other than" what they are experiencing now, in present day reality.

That discord, that mismatch between "what is" and "what they would like to be" creates suffering.

Now, you may ask: "How is that different from complacency? What about having a vision of what one would *like* to have?"

Here's the thing. I'm totally fine with having visions of what one may like to have in one's future. However, when that vision becomes the yardstick for how to measure one's success in life, one's happiness in life, that is a big problem.

Said another way, the tendency for most of us is to "identify" with that vision, to hold it in our minds to such an extent that it becomes who we are. We become so emotionally attached to that vision that we, in effect, become identified with it.

That is unhealthy.

Because when we do not meet that expectation that we have created for ourselves, we feel like we have failed. We have failed ourselves, and therefore we become unhappy and depressed. We suffer. This is not good. It is a result of not matching reality with what we desire. And taking what we desire too far.

How to manage this better?

"Turn within" regularly. Connect with oneself in a "non-content oriented way" regularly.

By doing so, we create a connection within ourselves that transcends the usual external desires we have. We naturally become more identified with our own mind in a less emotionally charged state, with our soul in a more expanded way than how we are in our normal focused awake state when we're walking around.

This builds an "insurance policy," so to speak, so we are insulated from becoming excessively wooed by the desires we may have. We become less likely to identify with them and less likely to define ourselves by those desires and visions of what we would like to have our lives look like.

And by relying on ourselves more, by acting from that more centered space, we act more effectively. In fact, we are more likely to be successful in making those visions and desires materialize.

We also create an insurance policy protecting us from any potential incursions into our Free Will by any, even well-meaning, spiritual teachers we may encounter over time.

Asking them questions, seeing if their answers make sense to us using our own common sense and our own "body of life experience." Not merely relying on their body of experience and *their* saying to us, "this is the way it is...." Because that is the beginning of the path labeled "Follow me blindly...."

And no spiritual teacher who understands spirituality and personal growth would demand that of any student. True spiritual teachers guide you to find your own way. To interpret your own experiences in your own way. To figure it out yourself.

Because that is the only way personal self-development can occur. Personally. Through oneself.

The Meaning Of Life

Don't worry. This is not going to be a traditional philosophy discussion. I fell asleep in my Philosophy 101 class in college, even sitting in the front row trying not to. I hope this essay has the opposite effect — and helps wake us up.

Many spiritual teachers speak about each of us having "a meaning to our lives." They use various terminology and explanations to describe this — words like dharma, duty, finding one's path, etc. But they all distill down to one basic fact: *someone else is telling us what to do.* Someone bigger than us knows better than we do. This notion that another mind or soul that is smarter or wiser than we are, and therefore knows better than we do what is good for us, and what we should be doing with our lives, is a theme that runs throughout spirituality. And I think it is a theme which does more harm than good.

THE GENESIS

It is the classic parental, paternalistic attitude towards raising children, isn't it? Those of you who are parents know exactly what I'm talking about. We sometimes think as parents that we know better, and sometimes we do, but not always. So, the issue is where do you draw the line if you are the parent?

In spirituality, this issue is no different. I think the parental or paternalistic attitude of many spiritual teachers towards their students over the millennia has given rise to this sort of attitude and has also resulted in certain beliefs just like this one — "the meaning of life."

I think somewhere along the way some very well-meaning spiritual teachers sought for their students what they thought would be best for their students and taught them about things like dharma, duty, following one's path, in order to help them along their way. But, in doing that, they may have helped the student in the short-term, but in the long-term I think they hurt the student by not allowing the student to "skin his or her knees," to live life fully and learn from their experiences, fully exercising their Free Will. "Free Will" meaning the ability to exercise all of their choices independently.

BEING COMFORTABLE WITH UNCERTAINTY

I think part of this paternalistic attitude by many spiritual teachers towards their students arises out of their concern for creating some sense of certainty for the student — the proverbial seeker along his or her path — to keep the seeker motivated. The reality of the "uncertainty of life" is often too much to bear for many seekers. Too daunting. And they quickly stop seeking in the way that the spiritual teacher feels is best for them.

So to motivate the student, the teacher has tended to choose short-term motivation techniques. For example, *creating certainty*. In this case the certainty of "knowing" that there is "a meaning" to the student's individual life. Even if what the teacher conjures up is not appropriate for that student. This sense of certainty is a built-in motivator to the student to keep them on the path that the teacher has created or envisions. It is the classic "carrot" motivator — "If you keep following my instructions, you will eventually discover the meaning of your life." That is the implication.

But is that truthful? The truly self-aware spiritual teacher knows that it is not accurate. Yet they feel that protecting the student from reality is the kinder, better choice. But is it?

BEING COMFORTABLE WITH THE UNKNOWN

Spiritual teachers who use that tactic in motivating their students are essentially telling their students, "Don't worry about the Unknown, because if you continue to follow my instructions, you will eventually find out — the Unknown will no longer be unknown to you." They are promising that you will know the meaning of your life if you believe in their school of thought, and follow their guidance and instructions. But again, does that implied promise match with the reality the student experiences? Does the Unknown ever become all known?

BEING COMFORTABLE WITH ONESELF

Instead, I think it is much more powerful, more accurate — and in the short and long run free from harm — to take the following approach.

Believe not in what someone else tells you to believe. Believe not in some other mind or soul's school of thought (whether they are on this side or the other side of the veil...incarnate or disincarnate). Instead turn within, go inside your soul, inside *your own* mind and figure it out as best you can at that particular moment in time. Be your own teacher. Become more comfortable with "your self."

Find and align yourself with techniques and teachers who espouse this sort of approach. *Run away* from the ones who want you to be their disciples, who want you to unquestioningly follow them.

Teachers are not bad. Teachers are necessary in our lives at various times. It is their *messages* that sometimes may be misguided due to either lack of understanding, or misplaced intent. As a student, that is what you need to look out for.

Being comfortable with oneself is the key to reducing the grip of fear that many of us have about the uncertainty of life, the great Unknown. As we increase our comfort, our understanding, our self-awareness, our knowingness with ourselves as individuals, we feel more secure inside, more self-confident, and the uncertainties of life loosen their grip on us, and eventually completely exit…leaving us free to live our lives fully.

And the technique for doing this is simple — turning within, knowing oneself, strengthening oneself from the inside out.

THE CONFUSION

Now let's talk about where I think the confusion may have arisen in some spiritual teachers' minds, when they talk about "knowing the meaning of life."

CHOICES A MIND CAN MAKE BEFORE BIRTH

As we have discussed in other essays, I think the individual mind or soul is much more powerful and expansive than most people give it credit for. I have experienced and observed, for example, minds making choices before birth, before coming into physical manifestation — before coming into their physical body.

We can make choices, for example, to accomplish certain things in our lives, to keep an eye out for certain friends we have encountered in other lives, to seek out and develop certain relationships. But these choices we may make prior to birth do not *guarantee* that they will happen. They are choices. They are not guarantees.

But, one could see how someone who is very self-aware and has experienced this sort of choice-making at that juncture in the soul or mind's development, and later became a spiritual teacher, could be inclined to teach their students that there is a "meaning to life."

I would say that that is a slight confusion or conflation of the experience. Instead, I think we make choices, and we may increase the *probability* of certain things happening by making certain choices, but that there is *always* the chance that we will make a *different* choice (for all sorts of reasons) that will give rise to different outcomes and consequences. There are no guarantees.

"SOVEREIGN MINDS"

So I would say it would be more accurate to say that we may have a *direction* to our lives based on certain choices we may have made before birth, but that there is no "meaning" to our life, since that implies a specific, identifiable, single choice that is not subject to change.

Moreover, I maintain that the approach that there is no "meaning to life" and that our lives are a collection of choices that we may make before, during and after birth that are constantly changing based on our own individual mind's ability to make more choices on an ongoing basis is in fact the *ultimate self-empowerment*. That there is no one "pulling our strings" — no one dictating to us what our life purpose is.

We make our own lives. We make meaning "in our lives." We may find meaning in our lives but it is not because we've found what some *other* mind decided *our* meaning to be.

To use a term that I refer to in my lectures, we are "*sovereign minds*" — we are free-standing individual minds with countless choices, controlled by no other mind.

That is the meaning of life.

"Free Will" Defined

I refer implicitly and explicitly to the idea of "Free Will" many times in my writings and talks. So I thought this concept deserved its own essay to clarify what we mean by it.

WHAT IT IS

"Free Will" means we each have *personal choice.*

Each mind has the ability to choose and make decisions on their own. Yes, we may sometimes be influenced by others, but ultimately we each own the ability to decide ourselves. On anything in life.

That's the definition of Free Will.

WHAT IT IS NOT

I have seen some spiritual teachers saying that Free Will does not exist because if it does, then they would be able to be expert tennis players (or millionaires, or whatever) just because they thought it into being. Free Will is not about "wishing" things into existence! It is not a measure of whether or not a desire will magically materialize! Those teachers are misstating what Free Will is. They utterly and completely misunderstand the concept.

As I said, Free Will simply means each mind has independent personal choice to make its own decisions.

NOT A MORAL ISSUE

We each make our own decisions. Period. To be clear, this is not a moral issue at all.

So Free Will should not be used as an excuse for not having social mores or laws. For example, you most certainly can make the Free Will decision to run a red light at an intersection while driving your car. Ignore the signal to stop — sure, you could make that conscious choice. However, there are consequences to that choice. In California, at minimum you could get a $500 ticket, or worse, depending on how serious the consequences to others were — if you seriously injured someone else by your action of choosing to run the red light — you could get jail time.

Are those social rules also made up by Free Will thinking minds in the local municipal government or state legislature? Absolutely yes. But we as a culture have also agreed using our Free Will thinking minds that running a red light is socially unacceptable (because it is unsafe) and should have social and legal consequences.

FAMILIAR EXAMPLE

Let me close with this example that most of us have seen played out in either our own or others' families — probably more times that we would like to count.

Does a 2-year old child have Free Will?

Even if the adults in the room — whether the parents, babysitters, aunts, or grandfathers — demand that the 2-year old child stop their temper tantrum, does that always work? Of course not. The child ALWAYS retains control of their own mind. They alone decide whether or not to stop the temper tantrum.

Now, if the child chooses to not stop, and continues their screaming fit, might there be consequences to that choice? Of course, yes. Depending on the conflict resolution skills and child-rearing beliefs of those adults in the room, there could be a wide variety of ways that child is handled.

Again, the point is that Free Will simply means we each have choices every moment of our lives. And no one — not even a powerful person who is 3 feet taller than us — can ever take away our ability to make our own decisions. Regardless of whether our decisions result in good or bad consequences for us.

Practical Benefits Of Free Will & Practical Problems Of Determinism

PRACTICAL BENEFITS OF FREE WILL	PRACTICAL PROBLEMS OF DETERMINISM
We can work it out (Beatles refrain)	We're stuck
Lots of possibilities	Limited options
Freedom	Trapped
Hope	Woe is me
Try again	Give up
Persistence	Abandonment
Life is generous	Life is a struggle
More	Less
Looking forward to the next challenge	What's the point?
Proactive	Passive
Choices	No choices
Nothing is figured out yet	Everything is already set in stone
Excitement	Dullness
New people, places, experiences	Same old same old
Seeking more	Settles for whatever
Happiness	Despair

Was It Meant To Be?

How many times have you heard that phrase?
Let's look at this more closely...

I love watching sports. When I was growing up, I played a lot of different sports — basketball, baseball, football, even some hockey. Now that I'm older and not into getting injured, I avoid all contact sports, though I still love shooting hoops, swimming... and watching football from the comfort of my living room!

But one thing I'm not fond of in sports is the frequent reference by athletes to "it was meant to be...."

And it's not a phrase that is unique to sports. We often hear it used by people in many life situations.

But, have you ever noticed that it is only used when athletes *win*? What's up with that? God or "destiny" only works when it's *in your favor*?

And when they lose, they'll often say, *"It wasn't meant to be...."*

What?

So, let me get this straight. The games are all fixed and someone somewhere already knows who's gonna win and lose? Someone better tell Las Vegas...!!

There is no "meant to be...."

There's only *"might to be...."*

That's what I like about sports. You need to play the game. Anyone can succeed. You never know. For me, it's a great 2-hour display of Free Will at work in a crucible for all to see. In front of 70,000 fans in a football stadium, with millions of viewers worldwide.

It is not predetermined. There is no "destiny"... otherwise you wouldn't bother to play the game, folks. And the bookies would make no money.

There is no "meant to be." There is only "might to be." Depending on the choices each player or coach (or referee) makes, a different outcome will be the result — in the game, at any given moment, during any given play.

And this isn't just true in sports.

It's true in life.

"SO WHAT," YOU MIGHT ASK?

The reason for understanding this more clearly is simple. When we get lazy in our thinking, we start creating false interpretations about how the world and our life operates, and when that happens, before you know it, we have created a whole set of false beliefs about ourselves and the world.

That inevitably leads to *unhappiness* because our expectations about ourselves and our world do not mesh. There is a major disconnect. And in large doses, people get depressed. In a word, unhealthy.

Instead, understanding more clearly leads to more accurate interpretations of the world and how our life works within that world, and then we create more helpful beliefs about ourselves and the world, which leads to more happiness for ourselves and those we come into contact with (because we affect them through our friendships and relationships).

FINAL THOUGHTS

Life is not predictable. There are *probabilities*. But there are no absolutes, no "definites." As much as we'd like that certainty in life, it doesn't exist.

So, that makes it incumbent upon each of us to "Be

prepared." Remember the Boy Scout motto?

Whether we're preparing for a sports game, or life as a whole...we need to be prepared. Both internally and externally.

Lots of experts exist worldwide to prepare people *externally* for the wide variety of games in life. The "Turning Within" Foundation is expert in preparing people *internally*.

Both are necessary to prepare us for maximum success in the game of life...to prepare us for whatever life throws at us... for whatever the "might to be" might be.

How The Belief
"It Was Meant To Be"
Causes Suffering

First, understand. It's a belief.
Not a fact.
It's a belief based on a desire, not based on factual reality.

And if you want to believe it, it's okay. I'm not here to change people's religious beliefs.

But if you want clarity in your understanding about reality and the universe, consider the following points. Then afterwards, perhaps reconsider whether your thinking that "It was meant to be," or the same idea expressed slightly differently, "Everything happens for a reason" is a belief based on reality or wishful thinking. And, moreover, whether it is a helpful belief.

"EVERYTHING"

First, when someone says "everything happens for a reason," the key word is "everything." That means there are no exceptions. It is an absolute statement.

"Everything" means every thing. Every occurrence. Every single thing that has happened, is happening, or will ever happen.

They mean by saying that, that everything is predestined. Everything in the universe that has already happened was already known (by somebody) that it would happen, and that somebody knows everything that will happen before it happens.

This concept or theory demands that Free Will, personal choice, does not and cannot exist in the universe.

Free Will and Predestination cannot coexist.

People who say they both exist are simply stating an illogical belief. It's like saying, "I am sort of pregnant." No. You either are. Or you are not. It is a binary fact. One or the other. You cannot be both pregnant. And not.

So again. If someone wants to believe that is true, they can. But it's not based in fact.

The same thing applies to those who say Free Will and Predestination both exist.

THE ALL-KNOWING SOMEBODY

What about this somebody who supposedly knows everything? And can predict everything?

Is that logical? Does that make sense?

This mind would have to be omniscient, all-knowing. And this has been the belief of many religions for millennia.

First, is it logical? Second, why does this belief exist?

It is a logical impossibility. Because "knowing everything" means every thing. Without exception. And therefore, knowing everything means that this mind must also know what it is like to "know nothing." Because "knowing nothing" is a subset of "knowing everything."

That is impossible. No mind can — at the same moment — know everything and know nothing.

CERTAINTY

But why do we create these illogical beliefs? Because we want certainty. And we would rather have the illusion of certainty than the reality of not having "an answer" — a catch-all answer.

Sort of a "Get out of Jail" card in the board game Monopoly. A free "hall pass" in high school.

But life isn't a board game.

It's a journey where Free Will operates. And not just *your* Free Will. But also the Free Will of quadrillions of other minds on Earth. Which are all influencing each other in ways that we cannot predict or know absolutely.

I get it.

When something terrible happens to us, we want an explanation. We want a reason. We think that will make us feel better. And it may.

Temporarily.

Until something happens that demonstrates that Free Will really does exist and that Predestination does not. (Remember they are each absolutes. No exceptions can apply.)

INCONSISTENCY & SUFFERING

But what do most of us do? We cherry pick.

We say, "See, look at this wonderful thing that just happened! It was meant to be!"

And we ignore the examples that show us that not *everything* is predictable. Not everything is within our control. We selectively choose our evidence to support our belief. We take the exceptions to be the rule.

But what happens when we take this inconsistent approach to our thinking?

We leave room for discord within ourselves. Logical and emotional discord. Suffering.

Our mind wants to understand. And our emotions want to feel good. We want to be happy.

The problem is the desire for immediacy. We are impatient. We want "drive-thru" spirituality. We want it quickly. We want it now. And we don't want to do much — if anything — to get it. Just believe and move on.

HAPPINESS

There is nothing amiss with the desire to be happy. I think it's why we are all here. Both on Earth now and on the Other Side later. And wherever we choose to go afterwards. And so on. It is all about the pursuit of happiness to me.

And I have found that — while it does take some additional work — logically thinking about life and the universe has brought me consistency in my thinking and thus emotional stability in my level of contentment. And thus my state of happiness.

Regardless of where the experience falls on the positive-neutral-negative spectrum.

And yes. Even amidst times of extreme sadness.

SUMMARY

So instead of trying to explain everything that happens in life by squeezing a square peg into a round hole, I suggest we accept life in the myriad of ways it presents to us. Enjoy those who are with us for as long as they are with us here. And know that nothing and no one can or is controlling everything.

That we are each Free Will thinking minds who are influencing each other — and who are being influenced by quadrillions of other minds at any given moment. So, yes, while *probabilities* do exist — nothing can ever be predicted with *absolute* certainty.

We each need to "turn within," relax, and gain a sense of inner security and confidence that replaces our seeming need for certainty with a desire to explore and experience the innumerable ways to appreciate the infinite wonder of life's eternal journey.

Everything Happens For A Reason?

Tell Neil and Jan Armstrong that when they ask you why their beautiful 2-year-old daughter Karen died of a malignant brain tumor.

Tell Marcus and Faustina Aurelius that about the 9 of their 15 children who died before age 10.

Or any of the other tens of millions of parents who have lost their children at any age.

There is not a reason for everything. Not literally.

Sometimes stuff just happens. Accidents or mistakes or "just stuff" that may cause an unforeseen physical abnormality in the fold of existence do occur.

It's called life.

And not everything in life needs an explanation or a "reason." Sometimes — I would argue all the time — life is simply happening.

Within us and around us. All the time.

And sometimes we can make sense of it. And other times we can't.

And that's okay.

We can be happy just living life. We should be able to be happy — contented — living our lives.

But most of us are not.

So we look outside ourselves for explanations for things that don't go the way we want them to. For reasons.

And we often make stuff up.

"Their baby died to teach them a lesson. To learn from. It

was a good opportunity for them to.... They may not see it now. But they will."

Really? ...How heartless.

How about accepting that nothing goes perfectly the way you want it to all the time? How about being less about trying to control our existence by explaining away experiences that cannot rationally be explained or reasoned away?

And especially if you are a spiritual teacher, isn't it a bit self-absorbed to think you can explain away every possible random experience in existence? Doesn't that imply omniscience?

I get it though.

We try to reason and explain everything — even, or perhaps especially, horrific events that are out of our control — in a vain attempt to maintain a semblance of order. Perhaps even to give comfort to another.

Because no one likes it when terribly unpleasant things happen, especially to good people.

But sometimes it does happen.

And I have found the most effective way to develop a sense of contentment with the inexplicable and the uncertain in life is to go inside. To strengthen my sense of self from the inside out.

To expand my knowledge about myself. Which in turn has expanded my acceptance of the world around me. With all its quirks, irregularities — and yes, its seeming mistakes.

Look around us. If we're truly candid, we see them all the time. And while we can "learn" from many of life's experiences, some of them just need to be accepted as part of the mix of life. Whether they are painful or pleasurable.

From the embracing of that realization...could come inner peace.

Destiny & Losing A Child

First, it is hard if not impossible to make sense out of losing a child to physical death before we, their parents, die.

Period. That is a given.

However, many parents who lose a child often ask me about "destiny" and whether they each had a role in crafting some sort of plan before birth that may have included the premature death of the child.

DESTINY

As for this idea of "destiny," you will see if you take my Afterlife & Reincarnation Experiences 6-part series, that I am a strong proponent of rational, demystified thinking. That yes, in my experience, the universe acts in a logical, understandable way. And that there are some basic fundamental principles that are consistent in our universe — on both this side and the Other Side.

FREE WILL

"Free Will" does exist for ALL minds. Without exception.

So, that means everything is subject to change *all the time*, given the potential *influence* of trillions of minds on each of us at any given moment. Yes, some of those minds have a more direct, and others a more indirect, influence on each of us, but ALL are influencing us all the time.

And, yes, *along with* the above principle, before we incarnate, we can have meetings with friends and others on the Other Side and "make plans" — or what some people call, "soul contracts." In other words, we can choose to think and plan strategically before we come back in a new life in a new biological body.

That said, not just our own changing of our minds, but more

importantly, the Free Will decisions by those trillions of other minds *will affect* our plans, especially as the plan unfolds.

So, yes, constant adjustment can be made, but we NEVER have *full* control over everything. No one does.

And I would argue *no mind* does…whether human, animal, angelic, god-like, or whatever other entity you want to label who has a "mind." Otherwise, you will have created an exception to Free Will, which I think does not exist.

So, if one wants to "label" that pre-birth plan as a sort of "destiny," fine. I'm okay with that as a loose metaphorical expression or term of art. But not literal. Not literally destiny, in the way most people think of destiny.

Because it is NEVER an absolute "pre-determined" plan or destiny with a *guaranteed* outcome (that is the way most people define "destiny"). That would contravene the idea of Free Will completely. You simply cannot have both at the same time (Free Will and Determinism are oil and water).

Period.

It is blatantly illogical — if you hear some so-called "spiritual experts" making such statements, it is a red flag. Cognitively dissonant. An attempt at putting a round peg in a square hole. Question it.

I am here to reduce fear in the world.

To do that sometimes requires undoing a lot of myths and illogical, cognitively dissonant thinking that, in my opinion, in the end can cause increased suffering in the world.

A CONSTRUCTION EXAMPLE

Using a construction project as an example might help illustrate this idea of destiny and Free Will.

Of course, the architect of the building is a key player in the project. You would be the architect of your "life plan." And the building project plans would be analogous to your choosing to plan your life with others — before any of you incarnated into your physical biological body.

However, so that the analogy more accurately mirrors real life, we need to also inject all the contractors, subcontractors, lawyers, accountants and investors/bankers into the equation (and many more — e.g., their respective wives, husbands, children, aunts and uncles of all of those people, etc.— you get the picture!!). They also ALL have an influence on the outcome of the construction project (post-birth).

So, to be thorough and realistic in our thinking and analysis, we also need to consider ALL the Free Will choices and decisions made by each of those many minds and the ripple effect — both direct and indirect — of those probably millions of choices. How all of those choices with varying degrees of influence impacted and perhaps changed the original architect's plan — the "pre-birth" plan that you may have had with your child who tragically died prematurely,

And so, at the end of the day, with such a complex interconnection and interaction with so many minds' choices, we might just as well end up having to say that your child's death is not able to be "figured out" — the unanswerable "Why did it happen?" That there may be no "reason" for it. Maybe you and s/he had a pre-birth agreement, but even if you did, with all the Free Will minds involved (NOT just yours and his/hers), the bottom line is that neither of you ever had *full* control over the outcome.

Life is about probabilities, not guarantees.

All we can do is act with what we know at the moment. Control and influence what we can. But we cannot foresee and take into account — much less "control" — every possible choice that every possible mind in the universe will make. Otherwise they don't have Free Will. And they all do. We all do.

As painful as it is to lose a child, I hope that perspective helps.

Has Spirituality Gone
To The Dogs?

A friend of mine just sent me an extremely troubling article about an investigative report aired today by an Australian news outlet, the Australian Broadcasting Corporation (ABC), on the serving of dog meat disguised as "chicken" in Bali to the thousands of tourists who flock to that purportedly "idyllic," tiny (95 x 69 mile) Indonesian island vacation and spiritual retreat hotspot. The Bali Animal Welfare Association (BAWA) estimates that 70,000 dogs per year are killed and served to diners there.

And, it is not the dietary choices being made by cultures around the world that is the issue. It is the methods used to capture, cage and kill animals — the cruelty and excessive pain and suffering inflicted on the animals that is most troubling, along with its matter-of-fact acceptance by the government and Balinese culture.

Those who label such cultures as bastions of spirituality are guilty of merely judging a book by its cover, without ever opening the book to read it. Being mesmerized by the number of temples and gorgeous natural landscapes, without looking deeper.

That article reminded me of my own experiences when I lived in a number of countries around the world. Many of them are considered by most people as "highly spiritual," and some have even been called "the spiritual centers culturally on the planet." I've often heard those very comments from friends as they boarded their planes to these lands far from the U.S. — phrases they may have read in travel books, and maybe even heard college religion professors pronounce.

But are they? Are they truly spiritually more developed?

Let's look more closely.

How does Bali — to pick one of many so-called "spiritually-labeled" countries — justify the cultural acceptance of capturing and killing of dogs (or in other cultures, cats or other animals) for food and then openly lying to tourists about the meat being "chicken"? Or worse, the inhumane treatment that often accompanies the sad ending of those animals' lives — the kidnapping, the poisoning, the lynching, the muzzling and suffocation in plastic bags, or the shooting? What does it matter whether they be dogs, cats, chickens or other animals? The cruel treatment is not justifiable. They each have minds and souls. They experience pain, fear and suffering. And let me say at the outset, that the fact that Americans may also treat animals poorly, does not justify the behavior anywhere in the world.

But we're not here discussing the detail of the treatment of the animals. We are here to discuss the level of spirituality of the culture.

And why do I think this is important, on a practical level?

I think it's important because so often Westerners travel tens of thousands of miles seeking spiritual sanctuary in places that they think are more spiritual than where they are coming from. The culture or place they are going to seems to attract them, putting them almost in a trance-like state as they book their flights to those far-off lands.

I have a different view of some of these far-off lands than most. I've witnessed this sort of in-your-face unethical behavior countless times as I've traveled the globe.

My experience has been that no matter how many temples, altars or public displays of reverence to ancestors, gods, or other deities that were on display in those countries, if you looked beyond those surface rituals, people were no different from the devout churchgoers in my hometown who professed much goodness, but often acted differently.

So, the lying about serving dog meat in Bali is unfortunately not surprising.

But there may be something that's actually worse than the lying that I don't think most Westerners realize.

When I worked for the President's office at MIT, one of the many seminars I taught there was on cultural differences. And how different cultures communicated and therefore meant different things when they said simple words like "Yes" and "No."

And looking through that cultural lens, what you realize — and arguably what may actually be worse and more troubling — is that many cultures do not see it at all as unethical or "cognitively dissonant" to tell an untruth — a lie.

In other words, they do not see a mismatch.

I find that is the most troubling thing. Because those beliefs and thoughts are the foundation for subsequent behavior. For actual physical acts.

Ethically, they often view money as the primary motivator even more than we do in the U.S. Ethically they would say it would be stupid for them not to fool you if they can get money out of you. So ethically, they consider that the most important part of the whole process. Have you ever wondered why piracy in China is so accepted, why it is so much an integral part of the cultural norm? Why stealing of other's intellectual property is so ho-hum normal? Why when you send your manufacturing drawings to them to build your factory, they are literally simultaneously building an identical factory a few blocks away to compete with your company?

And my experience has been that this phenomenon — this utter inability to see this issue as an ethical one — is not merely socioeconomic. In other words, it's not just poor people who think and act this way. It is a cultural norm in some countries, up and down the socioeconomic ladder.

And there is absolutely no connection between that and their view on spirituality which is often utterly based on how many candles, incense sticks or fruit they have brought to the altar in the middle of the town that day. As long as they have met the minimal requirements of their "spiritual duty and rules" as set out by some authority figure, they are "spiritual."

Sound familiar? No different from how many times a week you should go to church in the U.S. As long as you've met that minimum requirement, you can go home and kick your dog, then ask for forgiveness the next time you go to church.

In Bali, you lynch then eat your dog — in the U.S., you kick your dog. Either way, it is cruel and unacceptable. And obviously, non-spiritual.

I think it's a reflection of the lack of depth and perhaps the falseness of the "spirituality." And I think it stems from the false belief in Enlightenment in those parts of the world, where Enlightenment or "spiritual perfection" is viewed as a goal to reach at all costs. Or in the U.S., in the widespread belief in Heaven and that all sins can be forgiven if church is attended.

The ends justify the means.

That is the belief ultimately. And so the behavior in their daily lives reflects that. Of course this is not true for everyone, but I think it is the predominant belief among many in the East and many in the West.

That's the major spiritual mistake.

Westerners are easily duped by the physical number of temples, altars and prayer events. They mean nothing in reality. They are external trappings, mere symbols of cultures steeped in ritual acts, a reflection of the illusion of true spirituality that is often hyped as some sort of "spiritual tourist" marketing ploy.

Here's another example of the disconnect between spirituality and the external world.

I led a weekend meditation course for about 20 of my students hosted by a Buddhist monastery on Lantau Island when I lived in Hong Kong. I was a vegetarian at the time. To my surprise, when we arrived at the monastery and sat down for our first meal, all the dishes were full of pork and beef. More meat than I think I have ever seen at a regular, normal meal growing up in Boston, Massachusetts. No exaggeration.

When I asked our hosts, the Buddhist monks, why my request for vegetarian meals was not honored, they looked at me stunned, and said, "You are our guests, we want you to have what we cannot have."

So, essentially they were saying they would love to be eating pork and beef, but because the Buddhist rules dictate that they cannot, they do not. Was their spirituality being based on rules and being told what to do? Not based on what their inner voice was telling them they should do, or want to do? At least diet-wise, it seemed to be.

For me, as a young meditation teacher, that was an epiphanous moment. It showed me the illusion of spirituality, the depth of the illusion that exists in the world. If the Buddhist monks craved to eat meat and demonstrated their respect for me as their honored guest by serving me more meat than the normal American meat eater would eat in a given meal, that spoke volumes.

So when we Westerners travel 12,000 miles and say, "Amazing, Oooo, Ahhhh, Wow…" at how spiritually beautiful the culture appears on the surface — judging it by the number and beauty of the temples, the freshness of the flowers on the altars, and the frequency of the prayer events — let's not be the typical naïve Westerner blind to what is really going on.

Just because a culture seems "quieter" than our fast-paced Western culture does not mean the people are experiencing more "inner peace." Quiet behavior does not equal inner peace. And it most certainly does not equal spirituality.

As I said earlier, be careful not to be guilty of "judging a book by its cover."

There Is No Secret

Last night I watched a documentary on CNN
and was inspired to write this essay...
I literally started during the closing minutes of the film...

There is No Secret.

There is no secret to wealth or success — whether material or spiritual — in any aspect of our lives.

No one wants to hear that. No one wants to pay for a spiritual teacher to tell them that.

Everyone wants to know "The Secret." Remember that best-selling movie and book, "The Secret"? And remember all of those gurus in it who professed simple formulas for attaining all of your life's goals? Essentially distilled down to one message: "Think positively," or some similar mantra.

The thing is — people want to *believe* that there *is* a Secret. They want someone to tell them there is a Secret. They want confirmation that their hope is real.

And they will pay $10,000, $15,000, $20,000 — I know people who have paid $100,000 for a week-long course — to be part of that inner circle that learns that secret. That secret that gets them past their life challenges, that relieves them of that burden immediately. That secret that ensures they will experience enlightenment. That "break-through experience" that all those New Age gurus talk about. And all those prophets of antiquity spoke about. (You see, this is not a new phenomenon.)

Here is the truth:

The Secret is that there is no secret. There — I've said it. I've pulled the curtain back.

But people want an easy fix. People want "the Magic Pill." Especially people who are suffering, who are economically downtrodden, who are emotionally stressed. They have been the easy targets of gurus and prophets for 10,000 years — in Sumeria, Egypt, Judea, and India — and it is no different in 2016. In the United States. Europe. Asia. South America.

Look at how many self-development gurus have crossed Oprah's stage, how many of them she has proclaimed as "the savior of our society's ills..." There are legions, and here's the new twist in our TV and Internet Age — *they sell advertising* because many develop large followings. And followers are potential consumers. So, they get media attention, and more and more of us are lured in and seduced by the promise of the "easy, immediate fix." After all, Oprah said it's "the new secret."

Perhaps some of those you know have fallen into this trap — maybe even yourself. But, don't beat yourself up over it. Learn from it, and...

Ask yourself: Is that something we should continue to feed? That illusion that there is a Secret to Life?

I say No.

Especially those who claim to be spiritual teachers should be responsible, be transparent, tell it like it is. Guiding people by sharing perspectives with them is fine. It can be very helpful. However, encouraging blind following, listening without questioning — or even allowing it if one sees it happening — is irresponsible. It is that teacher's responsibility to explicitly and implicitly discourage guru following.

That said, there will always be those who will pay thousands of dollars for the magic pill, the secret. But the truly enlightened and responsible mentors, coaches, and teachers will not encourage or exploit those seekers. By doing so, those teachers are preying on the weaknesses that they, above all, should see clearly in those seekers and students. And that sort of conscious choice to take advantage of those weaknesses exposes such teachers for who they are. More materialistic than spiritual. More taking than giving. More snake oil salesman than spiritual teacher.

So, the lesson is that there is no magic pill. We each must find our own way in life, whether you believe that this is your only life, or if you believe that this is just one in an infinite series of lives. There is no secret answer.

And if you wish to truly seek a life that is more self-aware, more conscious inside yourself so that you may enjoy your life more fully, then you will best be served by a teacher or mentor who is a proponent of true "self-development" — as in the literal meaning of that phrase.

That we must each develop our "self"...that no one else can do it for us...and that there is no quick fix.

There is no getting around that.

And yes, we each should continue to pursue avenues that help us learn more about ourselves, facilitate our growth as human beings, as minds with conscious awareness, and Free Will in the universe. We just need to be careful to not give up our power to anyone else — no matter how "enlightened" he or she seems, no matter how "strong their energy, charisma or message" is. Trusting your "heart" does not mean dispensing with your rational mind. Use your common sense — to me that means your intuition, emotions *and* rational mind — all combined.

And we need to be patient and relax about all of this. Because based on my experiences, our minds or souls are eternal. Time is what we have plenty of. And we can probably never know everything about ourselves, but we *can* continue to learn more and more, because it will make our lives more enjoyable, more fun. Now, in the continual present.

That, I think, is the true secret. That there is no secret. No final answer. That we can reduce our fears, overcome our challenges, and *always* know more about ourselves and life itself. And this can increase our happiness and joy in our continuing conscious existence.

Dualism Versus
Non-Dualism

Why do spiritual teachers preach non-dualism? Why do they continually seek out and need to justify theories of "oneness" with — the Universe, God, the Absolute, pure consciousness, or other ideas? Why do they warn us to not be "confused" by dualism?

Why do they fear dualism?

UNFAMILIARITY WITH OUR MINDS

I think dualism simply confuses us because we don't have a full enough experience and understanding of *our own minds*.

People immediately jump to the conclusion that it must be "something other than myself" or "divine intervention" when they can't explain their unusual experiences. I've seen many people, often some of my clients who want to discuss their personal spiritual experiences with me privately, frequently make that assumption. After all, they say, how could "little 'ole me" have such a mind-blowing, far-reaching experience?

But as we each grow in our comfort and familiarity with our own mind, and how expansive it is and how diverse its experiences can be, we realize that those are experiences of our selves, not necessarily attributable to some one or some thing else outside of us.

With that realization comes the understanding that perhaps duality is not a bad thing — "duality" meaning the individual mind experiencing that which is outside of, distinct and therefore separate from it. In a nutshell: the experiencer is separate from his experience, thus the genesis of the term "duality."

Perhaps duality is actually an accurate description of what we have been experiencing all along — including those "far-reaching" spiritual experiences that often leave people speechless.

Moreover, the fact that we do exist separate and distinct from others does not dilute or negate our interconnectedness with each other. I would argue that not only does the realization not dilute the interconnectedness, it in fact can reinforce it. Because if we truly see and appreciate those differences, then we can appreciate the connection that much more.

And connection does not mean oneness. Oneness means sameness.

Seeing similarities and feeling familiarities is not "sameness." It is a conflation and confusion of terms when people describe their feeling of interconnection as "oneness."

Let's take a look at where I think that desire to describe it as "oneness" may come from.

LONELINESS AS A SOURCE OF CONFUSION

I think that the common jump to interpreting these genuine experiences of profound interconnection with oneself and others as "oneness" could stem from a deep emotional need many of us have. It could come from a loneliness that many people often feel within themselves. And so that "separateness" which is inherent in living life as a unique mind or soul, as each of us is, feels like an especially heavy burden when we are less connected within ourselves, and therefore we feel less confident, and less secure and centered inside. So, the knee-jerk reaction is to look *outside* of ourselves and look for this feeling of oneness with others because we don't feel a oneness — a deep connection — *within ourselves with our self.*

This is an understandable phenomenon, a natural reaction resulting from our deep inner disconnect. So, on the one hand, we should not beat ourselves up about it. However, we do need to recognize it when it is happening, otherwise we may find ourselves eventually addicted to any number of things — drugs, alcohol, gambling, buying stuff, relationship hopping, etc. — in our unsuccessful attempt at filling the internal void and loneliness with the external.

So it is important for us to recognize it when it happens, and why it happens. It is important because I think it can ultimately lead to our suffering which is not the objective of life. We are instead here for the pursuit of happiness.

The suffering occurs because when we don't experience that soul-satisfying "connection" through filling the void with external trappings, we become disillusioned, disappointed. And because our expectation is not met, that missed expectation causes us to suffer.

INSTITUTIONAL SOURCE OF CONFUSION

The other source of this conflation and confusion is more institutional. It comes from many, many thousands of years of teachings from spiritual teachers who have thought until recently that the goal of human life was to "merge with the oneness" — in all its various forms, depending on the spiritual tradition. This has given rise to all sorts of negative side effects.

For example, the denigration of living in physical form, the thinking that the body is lesser than the soul and therefore unimportant, the view that life on Earth is not really important and that the "Afterlife" is more important — Heaven, Nirvana, Enlightenment, or pick some other nomenclature from the many dozens of cultures or spiritual paths.

But, if the spiritual teacher communicating from the Other Side is being candid — and many are increasingly choosing to be more transparent — they will tell you that there is no "merging with any oneness." None of them has lost their individuality after they experienced their physical death. Even if they were well-established in their self-described "highly evolved" states of consciousness.

So the thinking has begun to change.

The thinking is that the mind is in fact eternal and its individuality continues eternally, its own self awareness in its own way. And that Free Will continues to operate unabated. That retaining our individuality is not only a gift, a good thing — since we can exercise our Free Will and make choices to experience life in the myriad of ways that it offers — but also because it is reality. And it is reality until experience tells us otherwise.

This is the new paradigm.

Dualism is not a bad thing. Dualism is reality.

The non-dualistic thinking was a theory that was experimented with, and it was decided to be discarded as a theory because the negative side effects of that theory were deemed to be too great, and after closer analysis of the theory, it was deemed to be inaccurate.

Said another way, it was decided that promoting "escapism" — escaping from physical reality and all that implies — which is what non-dualistic theories implicitly and sometimes explicitly promote — was not promoting the truth, nor was it promoting what is best for humanity.

It promotes not living in the present, not living life fully in the now. And hoping for something in the future that is complete and fulfilling — however, it turns out that is something that never happens.

It never happens because our "imagination horizon" is always just that — a horizon. It is always just beyond our thinking, our imagination. And since there is always something "just beyond," by definition we never reach it. So, by inculcating this notion of "oneness," this supposed non-dualistic reality, that exists "just beyond our imagination horizon," they had inadvertently created a cycle of suffering that lasts for eternity.

Not very appealing, right?

Instead, what is in the best interests of all minds is to promote the understanding of the independence and the interdependence of each mind. So that minds are encouraged to make their choices living fully in the continual present, and, at the same time, reminded to appreciate their connectedness — without confusing that with sameness or oneness.

To promote being *fully engaged* in one's life in the moment. Not looking for a way out. Not looking to escape to some "higher plane of existence" or to anywhere else.

Instead, to actually walk the talk, and live life and enjoy it *fully now.*

Wherever we may be.

Love & Self-Interest

Where does the notion that "we should not be self-interested" come from?

I think one source could be the angelic religion. Yes, there are a wide range of beliefs on the Other Side just as there are here on Earth, and while there is not one monolithic angelic religion, for the purposes of this essay, I will simplify the diverse angelic beliefs and just call it "their" religion.

How do they communicate with us? The conduits may sometimes be people who have had NDEs, psychics or mediums, or perhaps even direct communication with someone like you.

Keep in mind the term "angels" can refer to a wide range of beings on the Other Side — usually I refer to them as those who have never been incarnate in physical form, although some of you may consider your dead grandmothers to be "angels" as well. Both could be correct, since all beings over there are "beings of light."

And like many of us, some of these beings can become enthusiastic promoting their religious beliefs — which occasionally can even include worshipping them. In those cases, what better message to send to the humans than "you are not worthy," and "to be worthy, you need to not be selfish — and loving yourself is being selfish."

The implication being: "Instead, love (and worship, though they will not say that word) us."

Now, is this hidden agenda of "worshipping" true for all angels? No. Not all of them with whom I've communicated are out promoting their religious beliefs. And keep in mind, even those who are proselytizing — going "door-to-door" or in this case "mind-to-mind" — may genuinely think it's in your best interest for them to guide you in that direction.

They may sincerely believe they know better than you — how to live your life.

But for those angels who do that, that is often the first step to convincing humans not to self-love — that self-love is selfish. And instead, to convince humans that to love is to "first love others." Not yourself.

What does that message do? It creates insecurity. It undermines our self-confidence. It ultimately creates *dependence on others* for one's happiness.

And typically, when a "light being" talks to humans, those humans tend to listen. Because they often incorrectly assume the light being is "all-knowing." After all, you may say for example after your NDE, "But they showed me my 'life review'! It was amazing! How else could they do that? They must be all-knowing, or at least they know a lot more than I do!"

Yes. But we should not confuse *power with wisdom.*

And, perhaps more importantly, no one can look out for our self-interest as effectively as we each can ourselves.

My teaching is that self-interest is neutral. Neither positive nor negative. It just is. It is a universal reality.

So remember — that means that light beings are also naturally self-interested. They will tell you what makes them happy. Which might be following them. Worshipping them. Without any bad intention. As we said, they may actually think it is best for you.

But *do you?* Always ask yourself that. That's your self-interest talking. That's *you* looking out for *yourself.*

That's true self-love.

Don't allow anyone — whether they are a light being or a human — "take away" your independent ability to love yourself.

I put that phrase in quotation marks because, in actuality, you always have that ability. No one can ever "take it away." But you can sort of "give it away" by not exercising it.

Love is a powerful force in the universe.
Exercise it.
And first and foremost, exercise it for yourself.

Earth As A School To Learn

There is what I consider a false notion promoted by some minds from the Afterlife that Earth is some sort of "lower level" school for souls to learn lessons.

LESSONS

I think we "can" be here to learn lessons. But that is far different from "we must be here" to learn lessons. In other words, I do not believe that Earth is a "structural place in the universe" where souls are sent to learn lessons.

My experience is that the universe is structurally a much more neutral and egalitarian place than that. It is a place where we each can make of it what we want. That we as minds have Free Will, which means we have an infinite amount of personal choice in our decisions all the time.

LEVELS

First let's debunk the idea of "levels." Whenever I hear someone talk about "levels of evolution," "levels of consciousness," or "levels of learning," it makes me think about the principle that I call "The Importance of Being Important." That basic principle refers to the idea that many people think they are better than other people. Sometimes they even create third parties (God, gods, angels, ascended masters) who — they claim — judge them as better than others.

I think we do that when we are feeling insecure, not happy within ourselves, and therefore want to feel better, more secure. Makes sense, right? To do that, we often make others feel "lesser" than we are. By making those around them feel worse, the insecure unhappy person feels better.

Thus — "The Importance of Being Important."

I think this is something to guard against and to not encourage. Because it forms the seeds of cruelty. Where we may start to go down the hurtful road of deriving happiness from making others feel badly.

It's a slippery slope. Dehumanizing others by seeing them as "lesser beings" is an age-old tactic to make cruelty acceptable. Don't fall into that trap. Whether it's being promoted by someone on this side in the 1930's or from the Other Side in 2020.

So, when I say that I don't judge others internally, spiritually, in terms of "levels," does that mean that I see everyone as "the same"? No. But I do not judge other people internally from a spiritual level.

Why? Because I can't — I am unable to. As compared to whom? Me? I'm still always trying to figure myself out — I am an ever-changing being — so how could I ever "judge" someone else in that way?

How can I judge other people spiritually when I am on the Eternal Road of "figuring out myself?!" The road of Know Thyself.

Hypocritical, that would be? I should say so.

But as I have said in other writings, we can and should look at *behavior* and judge another person based on whether we want to be with that person, interact with that person, or not. We always have that choice, that ability to exercise our Free Will with the goal of increasing our happiness. Moreover, making those types of assessments of other beings based on their behavior, and acting on that by sometimes drawing boundaries between them and ourselves may be a very wise decision.

But that is not the same as judging another person's *internal* state of being.

MORE LIFETIMES — THE SMARTER WE GET?
What about this common idea in spiritual circles?

"Don't we get smarter, more evolved the more lifetimes we have on Earth? Aren't we here to eventually graduate from the Earth school?"

First, let's address the lifetimes thing. Yes, I think many of us have been here for many lifetimes, and some of us out of the 7.6 billion humans on planet Earth today in 2020 have not been here for very many human lifetimes. Does that mean the ones who have been here for many lifetimes are automatically "smarter," "more evolved," or "more developed intellectually, emotionally, or spiritually"?

I think that is actually an easy question to answer.

Absolutely not.

The number of lifetimes one has had as a human on planet Earth (or on other planets) does not necessarily mean you are smarter in any of those ways. Because how smart we are is dependent on whether we are paying attention or not.

And over the hundreds of thousands of years — perhaps millions of years — that humans have been on this planet, most of those lifetimes have been spent in what we might call "survival mode." Gathering and collecting food, finding shelter, warding off predators and disease — enough to keep us alive. Surviving.

And when I have been in survival mode even in this lifetime as Kelvin Chin, I definitely recall that it has been more difficult for me to be "self-aware," "loving," or "thinking of others."

If we are candid, I think we would all admit that when we are in survival mode, that's what happens to us. We become all-consumed with living moment to moment. Self-reflection becomes a luxury. Not a "must have." That makes learning from our life experience very difficult. Even unlikely.

So, I don't think it is a foregone conclusion that merely because one has had many lifetimes on this planet, that one has become by that mere fact — by default — a more evolved human being.

Is the number of lifetimes as a human being a factor at all? Yes. However, I think the more meaningful question is this. How many lifetimes has one had in a *non*-survival mode, where it is more likely that one has had the mental and emotional freedom — the flexibility — to be more self-reflective and self-aware? That is the more important factor than "number of lifetimes."

Second, why are so many people so eager to get off of planet Earth? To supposedly "graduate"…and go where? To the non-physical realm? Why not enjoy the beauty and physicality of being here while we're on this planet with its dense physical vibration? Enjoy the sunsets. Enjoy being in our dense physical biological bodies — the feel of movement, the smell of it. Something that many of us will miss, I guarantee you, when we're on the Other Side. Enjoy the feeling of water on our bodies when we're taking a shower or bubble bath. Enjoy the taste and feel of soft serve ice cream in our mouths — it simply is not the same when we don't have a physical body!

ENJOY...AND PERHAPS CHOOSE TO LEARN

Enjoy life. Whether we're on this side or the other.

And when life here gets difficult, which it sometimes does, work through it. Use it as an opportunity to experiment. You might even say "learn from."

"But wait," you might say — "I thought you said you didn't think Earth was a school?!"

Yes. Not a structurally created school.

But, in my experience, Free Will operates throughout the universe. And that means we *can* exercise our Free Will to "choose to learn" while we are here on Earth (or anywhere else for that matter). That's my suggestion and what I choose to do.

But it's a choice. Not an order from above.

Angels & Fear

There seems to be increased activity among some angels on the "Other Side" whenever a perceived crisis happens on planet Earth. Whether that be a World War, the end of a millennium or even the end of a century — 1699, 1799, 1899, 1999.

Now, it seems to be COVID-19, which should not be a surprise. After all, it is a global pandemic affecting all humans on planet Earth.

For those who pay attention to such things historically, such times tend to be "ripe" for concocting messages around those events which supposedly predict the "end of life on planet Earth" (the same thing happened when AIDS was first identified in the 1980's).

Impending apocalypses are routinely aimed at provoking fear among those humans prone to being fearful — which unfortunately is most of us!

Now, 7.6 billion people.

And my observation is that many tend to use that hotbed of fear to promote ideas that are often self-serving. That includes minds on this side AND minds on the Other Side — yes, including some angels.

By the way, do not assume any being on the Other Side knows more than you do. Not necessarily so. Some may. But the fact they are a "light being" is meaningless when you are assessing that mind's wisdom — after all when we die, it becomes clear we ALL are light beings. Think about that.

As many of you know, my work over the millennia and now again this lifetime is to *reduce* fear in the world, especially but not limited to — the fear of death. That said, my goal is always to help people live their lives more fully *in the present*, regardless of their beliefs about death or dying — cultural or religious — and whether they believe in an "afterlife" (the Other Side), or not.

In addition, I take a rational approach toward looking at life. And that includes a rational, logical approach towards interpreting any experience we may have. That rational way of analyzing life has served me well in developing understandings that are cognitively *consistent*, not cognitively *dissonant*. And that has been the foundation of my happiness over the millennia.

So, I have a few thoughts about the current messages that seem to be floating about the social media airwaves on 2020 planet Earth.

MESSAGES IN DREAMS OR OTHER VISIONS

There seems to be an uptick in messages purportedly from the Other Side that portend a dire, almost cataclysmic future in the coming months and years. Keep in mind — these messages ALWAYS seems to happen when there are crises on Earth.

Such messages may come in the form of lucid dreams, visions or messages through psychics or other mediums. They can be visual, audio, telepathic or in some other form of communication, e.g., symbology, etc.

As I have mentioned in some of my lectures, I had messages from the Other Side come to me in 1986 about how quickly humankind needed to move more positively, otherwise.... For some reason, an inherent threat always seems to be included in that sort of fear-based message.

And of course, the messages always seem to have enough "general kernel of truth" in them to be considered somewhat accurate in hindsight, even if their overall specific message ends up being false (e.g., "mass chaos with foreign armies in the streets" — that's one that is floating around now in the social media circles in mid-2020).

SOURCES OF THE MESSAGES

These messages from the Other Side can come from various sources.

All of these sources are technically "light beings" because *everyone and everything* is made of light — in fact, that is true whether we are talking about on this side OR the Other Side. Sometimes we may actually perceive reality in this way. Other times we may not. However, fundamentally, we are all "light beings."

I think confusion often arises when someone experiences a communication from the Other Side, and forgets that fact.

Sometimes the communications are from dead relatives or loved ones (they may tell us who they are). And often we recognize something about their personalities (maybe their word choice, unique sense of humor, perfume, or other identifiable trait), so we may have some external evidence of who they say they are. Other times, even though they may simply appear to us as a "light being" — they may "show" us a recognizable face or a bodily form we may recognize. So, "light beings" could be any of those sources or take any of those forms.

Other times they may come from "light beings" we don't personally recognize. For example, they may simply appear as a generic orb of bright luminescent light. This is when people typically jump to conclusions.

The most common interpretation of these "light being" experiences is almost always filtered through that person's religious or cultural beliefs. So if someone is a believer in God, they typically interpret that "being" as "God." That is the most common default.

Sometimes they may instead call the "light being" a spiritual being they worship or respect — Jesus, Mohammed, Buddha, Archangel Michael, Shiva, or perhaps some other entity they are familiar with.

You get the idea.

The person filters it through their own mind and bases it on their past experience having known the person, or if not, then bases it on their belief system.

So, what's my point?

When you hear a psychic or preacher say the message they are telling you is from "God," "an archangel," or whomever, don't blindly believe them. Even if they ardently believe it themselves.

Belief does not mean truth.

CONTENT OF THE MESSAGES — PREDICTIONS?

Whenever you hear someone say they are "prophesying" something, or that they can foretell the future, BE SUSPECT of everything they are saying.

Why?

Because anything that smells of "predicting the future" violates the fundamental universal principle of Free Will.

Free Will means we have personal choices we each can make. And because of the 7.6 billion human minds on Earth (and that's not counting all the dogs, cats, horses, etc. who also have minds and therefore can influence our choices), no "future" can be predicted with absolute certainty.

If anyone claims to predict the future with certainty, you know they either 1) don't know what they are talking about, or 2) have a hidden agenda and are trying to fool you into following them. Either way reveals someone whose thinking should be at least questioned, and perhaps not trusted.

The future is based on the continual present. And our

present is obviously based on many choices that not only each of us is making, but also all of the other free-will thinking minds on Earth are making.

We each INFLUENCE each other. We do NOT *control* each other. But we do affect each other's choices. Therefore, nothing can be predicted with certainty. No future is absolutely predictable.

Yes, we can predict with some level of "probability" — the *likelihood* that something will happen. But never with absolute certainty.

So, can someone get a message from this side or the Other Side saying that things on Earth may get messy in the coming months. Sure! But it would not take a rocket scientist — never mind a psychic or someone on the Other Side — to tell us that. The probabilities of it getting messy during this worldwide COVID-19 pandemic and U.S. presidential election year are obvious.

Do not buy into the fear inherent in that message. That is what they *want* you to do.

Why, you may ask?

ANGELIC AGENDAS

When I first started having communications with the Other Side in 1986, the initial communications were with angels and archangels. I soon discovered that many of them were more interested in my promoting their angelic beliefs on Earth than helping me with my own personal self-realization, so we each moved on. But I learned a lot from those two years communicating with them.

Why would angels want to convince humans that the Earth is in danger?

My experience is they have minds just like we all do. And as such, they have desires and emotions — hopes, dreams and expectations. Sometimes that comes with an agenda. Maybe even a hidden agenda.

First of all, understand that the angelic realm is not monolithic. That means they — like us — do not all believe the same thing. For example, the cadré of angels who hang out with me now are more "independent thinkers" — they tend to have their own ideas and beliefs about things, and are not followers of the masses of angels.

Did I say "masses" of angels? Yes. Just like on Earth, there are "the masses." What does that term mean?

Well, think about it. It's no different than here where you and I live — on Earth. There is the way most of the human population live and think, and we call that "the masses." On the Other Side where angels live, there are also the masses, where most of them think and believe more or less similarly.

I would say most of the angels are there to help humans move forward in a more positive direction. However, might there be other angels who have less altruistic intentions?

Sure. Like I said, they are minds just like we are.

WHY WOULD AN ANGEL PROMOTE FEAR?

Let's say an angel was promoting a fearful message of "the future" through a preacher or psychic on Earth. What would be the self-interest for an angel to do that?

Followers.

Followers to add to their flock on the Other Side. If you have that as your goal, why not start recruiting those potential followers while they are still on Earth? And while you are at it, why not create dependence *on those angels* as the "spiritual leaders" who can guide you away from the fearful situation they are predicting.

That is the hallmark of any religious cult — develop

dependency among the followers on the leader or leadership. Suppress independent thinking. But make it all about "helping" the followers move along their spiritual path.

Understand that historically, this is exactly what Paul, also known as "Saul of Tarsus," did 2,000 years ago after Jesus was murdered.

Religious historians who have read Paul's original letters in Greek all agree that Paul was a promoter of the apocalypse — he was preaching that the "end of the world" was going to happen (the written records show he prophesied and stated) "within 6 weeks." He openly discouraged people from buying property or marrying, and instead told them they should be unquestioningly following him and the belief he created, and if they did, they would be rewarded by skipping to the front of the line to get into heaven.

Lots of people signed up. Many still are.

My suggestion: don't be fooled by that well-worn, commonly-used spiritual recruitment song:

"Be afraid, be afraid.
Follow me, follow me.
I will save you, I will save you."

What song is that? I don't know. I just made it up. But you get the idea.

You have seen it sung before over the millennia, I am sure.

ALTERNATIVE CHOICE

Instead, how about choosing to "follow yourself"?

Why not trust yourself — do what you can to strengthen yourself by "turning within." The "inside out" approach.

Don't always look to others and blindly do whatever they say — do what makes sense to you.

And if you do choose to listen to a psychic or preacher, I

suggest that you still continue to ask yourself whether what they are saying makes sense. Does it pass the "common sense" test?

Moreover, even if you do believe their predictions about dire things happening in your near future, why follow their advice to hoard food and buy guns? Doesn't that sound like a fear-based approach to life?

"Build a fort. And defend it." Really? Is that the motto you want to live your life by?

How about instead inspiring others to find solutions to problems that have existed for hundreds of thousands of years among human beings?

Are you helping solve the problems? Or are you simply adding fuel to the fire of fear?

JUDGE THEIR BEHAVIOR

My advice is to always judge others by their behavior. Not by what they say they are going to do. But what they *actually* do.

Ask yourself — is the psychic, spiritual leader or angel who says they are "not promoting fear but are here to help humankind on Earth" walking their talk? Do their words match their actions?

If you find they do not, then find a different source of advice.

Online Dating With Angels

Think about it.

Isn't going to a psychic or medium who may connect you with a dead relative or even an angelic being really a form of online dating?

Okay, it may be spiritual in intent, and not relationship or sex based. I'll give you that.

But I'm not talking about the objective or goal of the session or connection. I'm talking about *the process*.

Let's look at it.

You go to a psychic, or maybe you can even close your eyes and connect with "the Other Side," the "unseen world" all by yourself. Cool. And then what happens?

Either someone, the psychic, or some other mind from the other side of the veil, tells you that you are talking or otherwise communicating and connected in conversation with a nonphysical, ethereal being — let's for sake of simplicity here agree to just call them "angels."

Okay. Got that?

What is going on from a process standpoint?

You are now in contact with someone — here, an angel — who says they are an angel and may describe themselves in certain ways. A certain perspective on humans, on the Earth plane, maybe they describe how tall they are, how big their wings are, what color or energy vibration they are. All of that.

But what is the underlying factor in all of this?

You TRUST them. You either trust the psychic, or you are trusting yourself that this is in fact an angel talking with you.

Sound familiar? Sounds a lot like…

Online dating.

Right?

Just in angelic form.

Isn't it just like checking out a profile on an online dating website, then contacting that person? Do you see them in person? No. You *trust* that the person on the other end of the email or text message is who they say they are. Maybe you do a video chat.

But how do you know for sure? You don't. That's the point. Maybe they are a 6'2" tall guy, or a woman who is a fitness and yoga instructor, or maybe he's really 2" shorter than you and is 5'6" tall, and she used to be an instructor…but 20 years ago.

At least in online dating you can find out. You can assess the credibility, and say, "Hey, let's meet at Starbucks tomorrow," and you can see them in person. See if they are real.

Not just some fake banker in Nigeria (a guaranteed no-show at Starbucks unless you are dating in Nigeria), or the widow of Yasser Arafat trying to get your bank account number (yes, no joke, I got that one today, an email sent to my Overcoming the Fear of Death website!).

So, what's the point?

My point is that regardless of how trusted your psychic is, or how strong your ability to connect with disembodied entities is, check them out. Check out the angel, just like you would your online date.

Okay, granted. You may not be able to see them in person. You may not be able to tell your new angel friend to meet you at Starbucks, but check out what they say to you, what advice they give you. Does it make sense?

Use your own mental, emotional, intuitive faculties to assess their credibility.

Do NOT take what they say at face value just because they

are without a physical body. Not having a physical body just means they don't have to eat food like we do. It doesn't guarantee them some sort of exclusive rights to wisdom or good advice.

Think of it this way — would you (or did you) automatically drop everything you're doing and listen to exactly what your parents or grandparents told you every time they spoke? No. Well, after they died and maybe became angels or other disembodied entities, why would you listen unquestioningly to them then? Same minds, just no bodies.

So, I'm not saying to ignore what angels may tell you. I'm just saying don't assume they are always right about what they're saying. They may have an agenda, even unconscious, based on beliefs they have developed over the eons. Those beliefs may be accurate, or not. Helpful, or not.

Make up your own mind after you hear the messages. After all, would you believe everything a stranger told you on an online dating site?

Unbundling Enlightenment

The idea of "Enlightenment" has been tossed around in spiritual and philosophical circles for the past 10,000 years on this planet. Let's look at it, dissect it, and see if we can understand it more clearly.

My goal in doing so is simple: To live life more fully now, in the present.

First of all, let's clarify what we're not talking about. If you use the term enlightenment to mean self-aware, understanding yourself more deeply or clearly, or "knowing yourself" — that is not how I'm using the term "enlightenment." Those are all very practical and useful pursuits that I encourage.

I'm using the term in the way that most spiritual seekers use it. Most often it means some advanced state of consciousness, some state of awareness where the person has achieved some state of so-called perfection. "Acting in accordance with the laws of Nature," "Right action" are terms that one often hears associated with it. Enlightenment implies a state of full "can't-grow-anymore" self-awareness. The alleged pinnacle of human evolutionary development. Such seekers are seeking a stated "goal," not seekers of eternal growth.

It is primarily associated with Eastern religions and cultures, but thinking and belief in this concept is not isolated to Asia. There are many references to it in Western culture — in Greek philosophy, Judeo-Christian theology, and many other traditions and cultures. I'll let you research those on your own, but let's continue with our analysis.

PERFECTION?

Recently I saw in the *Atlantic* an article and video revealing the collapse of yet another cult. It posed the issue of why seemingly intelligent people would get fooled into dropping everything and following a self-proclaimed "enlightened" leader.

What is this "perfection" that these followers seek? Is it real? Does it even make sense?

The first thing that jumps out at me is that the idea of perfection means that there's nowhere else to go after that. If you are perfect, there's no need — or opportunity — for improvement. That means you have plateaued out, you have reached a static state. No change after that. The end.

Most cultures and religions that have this belief in enlightenment justify that lack of continued growth, that state of "no more change," by saying the individual then "merges" with something else. God, Source, the Absolute (which, in their belief systems, is considered "non-changing"), or some other similar concept.

Is that practical and useful?

BEYOND THE IMAGINATION HORIZON

I think the concept is neither practical nor useful. It creates a subtle "under the surface but there" attitude in the believer that life is not really worth living until one has arrived at that future state — enlightenment. It pulls like an undercurrent of energy at the person's thinking that constantly, again sometimes very subtly, distracts them.

That is not living in the present. Instead they are living "beyond the imagination horizon." They are always imagining what their life *could be* if they were enlightened, if they were "perfect." Instead of living in the present and enjoying their life, they cannot stop thinking about what it would be like living at some future point, beyond their imagination horizon.

Does this mean you shouldn't have hopes and dreams? No,

of course not. Having a vision of your future, *what you would like to have,* is healthy and normal. That is not what I'm talking about.

I'm talking about something extreme. Yes, it can express itself sometimes in very obvious ways, and other times more subtly. Yet all such believers focus their life on something that is beyond their present grasp. Some may sell all their worldly possessions, give up relationships, and perhaps even blindly follow someone who promises perfection. Others are more subtle about it, perhaps eschewing the physical ("the body is just a food machine...") in favor of the non-physical etheric.

UNETHICAL BEHAVIOR

This idea of enlightenment "at all costs," also encourages the life strategy of "the ends justify the means." Or in the vernacular: "Anything goes." Because the goal is perfection, the individual internally more easily persuades him/herself that any action is "in accordance with right action" or "everything I do is the will of God, even if it is criminal" if it somehow is related to the pursuit of perfection (or merging with God).

Fallacious thinking that leads to people "bending the truth" to fit the circumstances because the lofty goal of enlightenment trumps all can often be the outcome. Thus, even lying becomes acceptable because it is "for the greater good."

The real-life examples are many — see the history of the collapse of any cult.

SUFFERING

This "Living in the *Non*-Present" also has a serious unintended consequence. It leads to continual suffering. The individual constantly is unhappy with their present situation, their present condition in life. They always seek something that is beyond their grasp. This ensures an unhappy life.

261

And does that idea of perfection even match people's experience?

PEOPLE LIKE YOURSELVES

Does this idea of a non-changing experience of perfection or enlightenment match the experience of anyone you know, or even of yourself?

The experience of deep and profound connection within oneself can be a very real experience. And this experience — or set of experiences — may even be difficult to articulate, to put into words that can "do it justice." But often the individuals who have this experience immediately jump to the interpretation that they are enlightened or are experiencing a "divine experience" of some sort. I think this is misplaced.

This misinterpretation understandably arises because that experience is so different from what I call the "supermarket aisle" state of the mind that we are so used to — that part of our mind that is constantly making decisions ("should I get peanut butter, chunky or smooth?") — that we jump to interpreting that experience of deep inner connection as something "outside of ourselves." As I've alluded to in other essays, this is due to our fascination and attachment to the "Conscious of XYZ" model of viewing life — we view life and assess life based on the specific, identifiable objects that we experience, the XYZ's.

And, even when you do have that deep inner connection, you are *still aware*. You don't blank out. (If you do blank out, I think it is because of some inner fears that, because of our self-regulatory system, shut your mind down, not because of some "cosmic experience.")

Moreover, if you are still inwardly aware — the proverbial "light is still on inside" — then "somebody is still home." You. *You* are still home. Your individuality is still intact, albeit in a form that is very much NOT like the "supermarket aisle" mind that you are so used to.

Now, let's look at the personal experience of some of the well-known spiritual and philosophical figures in human history…

So, I'm warning you — the next section may get a little "far out" for you so if you believe that communications with "the Other Side" can and do occur, continue reading.

If you don't, no problem. You can stop reading here because the above thinking should be enough to cause you to pause and reflect, and see if it makes sense to you. At least it should cause you to pump the brakes a bit if you have found yourself "blindly following" some spiritual teacher, perhaps even unintentionally.

If this essay has caused you to rethink your decision to blindly follow another's beliefs, then its objective will have been met. It will have allowed you to realign yourself within yourself, so you can reclaim your own power over your life and enjoy it more fully now in the present.

But for those of you who are still with me, let's discuss some of the spiritual luminaries in Earth's history and their experience with this idea of Enlightenment…

WHAT ABOUT JESUS, JEHOVAH, SHANKARA?

Jesus, Jehovah, John the Baptist, Shankara, Yogananda and Plato have all recently come to a similar conclusion — that enlightenment as a state of perfection is illusory and does not exist.

Here are the takeaways that they have shared:

None of them have merged with the supposed Oneness, Absolute, or God.

That we are Eternal minds. And as such, we always retain our individuality, our individual awareness of ourselves as we continue on, each in our unique life journeys. (See 30thNovember.com for more on this.)

THE ETERNAL MIND

Is life eternal?

Many people believe that life is eternal. For example, some may think of eternal life as other lives continuing after one dies, i.e., life on the planet still continues after one's death — they may view themselves as non-eternal, but that life in the form of *other people's lives* will continue after they die. To them, this is a form of eternal life, where there is still conservation of the energy that was their life, in the form of others who may come after them.

Yet other people may believe that *their own lives* may continue on after death — the idea of an "afterlife" like Heaven, or perhaps even reincarnation. In that latter belief system, there is a belief that the energy continues and the personality may also continue afterwards in yet a different physical form, a different body and a different lifetime.

The First Law of Thermodynamics states that: "Energy can be changed from one form to another, but it cannot be created or destroyed. The total amount of energy and matter in the Universe remains constant, merely changing from one form to another."

Essentially, it says that we are energy. Yes, we have bodies, but even our bodies are made up of energy — molecules, atoms, other small particles.

So, if our energy cannot be created or destroyed, perhaps we simply change form. We may debate, depending on what our belief system is, "what form" we change into. But, the First Law of Thermodynamics seems to indicate that energy is not lost — because no energy in the universe is gained or lost. It is the same energy that has always existed.

In any of those cases then, where the belief is that life is eternal, there can be no beginning or end. Because that is the very definition of "eternal."

FINAL THOUGHTS

Since the First Law of Thermodynamics along with a growing number of people's experience indicate that our minds (synonyms: soul, awareness, consciousness) are eternal, and that we can choose to (or choose not to) come back in another lifetime as often or as many times as we like, the advice is to relax. There is plenty of time. Enjoy the journey. Stop trying to fit it all in.

Dispense with all fears, including the Fear of Missing Out (FOMO) — that many young people in the world have.

Live in the continual present because that is actually all we ever have. Stop living in the illusion beyond the imagination's horizon. And enjoy our friendships and relationships with the knowledge that we can and will likely meet again.

Karma Unbundled

I will cut to the chase.

The whole notion of "karma" was a made-up theory by a group of Vedic spiritual leaders about 10,000 years ago. And "dharma" too. (See 30thNovember.com for details about the group and the creation of their theories).

WHAT WAS THEIR INTENT IN CREATING THESE THEORIES?

Essentially to help move humankind forward by prodding us to act more kindly, with fewer human sacrifices (ideally, none), and to be less lazy in our behavior and actions. That's the reason in a nutshell. Again, see the above-mentioned talk if you are curious for more in-depth historical details.

But, back to the theory itself...

So, are there consequences to our actions? Is there karma in that sense? Absolutely yes. Everything we do has consequences.

But there's no cosmic "accounting system" of "rewards and punishment" given out by some tribunal of godlike judges or by some innate omnipresent energy force (sometimes people will call it "the Universe" or "Mother Nature" or "Source").

In other words, karma is not *structural*. It's not some independent eternal universal concept — it was a theory made up by a small group of well-meaning spiritual leaders about 10,000 years ago to curb human sacrifices and other extremely hurtful behavior. And then over the millennia, the theory got twisted, conflated and added to by other religious and spiritual leaders who sometimes had a less altruistic intent — instead, a desire to have more power over others, or to even directly control the behavior of others.

To the point now where billions of people believe they amass "mountains of karma" that may take them millions of lifetimes to get rid of...and that's only assuming they don't accumulate any more "bad karma" on a daily basis (which of course they think they are doing)! So they are left distraught, defeated and depressed. Constantly living in fear and unhappiness. Afraid to live life for fear of making the "*millions* of lifetimes" become "*billions* of lifetimes"...

All the while not realizing it was just a theory to start with. Not a pronouncement of some supposed structural universal principle.

Creating debilitating fear in the human race was certainly not the consequence intended by the creators of the theory 10,000 years ago.

THE PERCEIVED NEED FOR CERTAINTY

Why has this "blind" belief in the idea of karma — which has risen to an almost religiously-fevered pitch worldwide — become so popular?

Because people want certainty. And they want certainty because their level of inner security demands it. Because we are essentially *disconnected within ourselves* and therefore insecure, lacking in inner strength.

So we grasp at anything — yes, even a theory like karma — a theory that if we examine it more closely is fear-*inflating*, and so it really is not in our best interest. But it seems to give us certainty. It gives us a rule to follow — "Don't do bad stuff or you will get punished with bad karma. Do good stuff and you will get rewarded by chipping away at your pile of bad karma with your good karma."

And following that rule is seemingly easier than figuring out within ourselves what makes us happy and basing our choices on that. Because that involves "turning within" as well as each of us looking at our individual desires and emotional patterns

— oooooh, way too much work! So, instead we blindly follow some rule.

And that rule — which started out 10,000 years ago merely as a theory — is perpetuated.

FREE WILL

Looking at this old theory about karma more dispassionately, it also contradicts Free Will.

Free Will means "freedom of choice to make any decision one wishes." That means hurtful or helpful decisions. And, hurtful or helpful to anyone — oneself...or to others.

And if that's the case, it means without restriction. Good or bad. That's what Free Will means. Otherwise it's not "free" will.

Again, I'm talking about this from a *spiritual* standpoint. Not social. Socially, we may decide to have laws or codes of conduct that forbid certain unacceptable, hurtful behavior. I leave that to the social scientists to decide what and how best to manage our social behavioral issues. So I am not suggesting we should have no prisons for bad actors in our society, nor am I debating whether that is the best means for curbing their bad social behavior.

Instead, I am talking about this spiritually. And the social issue of having societal laws to follow is not the same as an eternal individual soul "amassing mountains of good or bad karma."

And looking around for even a split second, we can all see examples of the existence of our Free Will. Our ability to make personal choices — even to disagree when told to do something and to make the opposite choice.

Has anyone ever observed the behavior of a 2-year-old child?

So since Free Will clearly exists — we can make any choices — which also means we can make good or bad choices — it does not fit alongside the (now) old theory of karma, which implies some universal knowingness and judgment of what is "good and bad." If we then agree that Free Will exists, the theory of karma must be the incorrect of the two ideas.

RANDOMNESS OF LIFE

Life is much more random than most of us realize, or would like to admit.

Yes, we do make our own individual choices. And yes, we should make those decisions in as informed a way as possible, and try to take control of our lives as much as we can. Think and plan ahead as best we can. Of course that is true.

However, we must also be equally aware of this unmistakable fact in life: everything is not within our control. Nor is it even possible that everything would be able to be within our control.

Why?

Because many other minds are always involved, known and unknown, in our lives. Directly and indirectly. Seen and unseen. And their Free Will is always operating — their inherent right to have varying desires and their innate ability to act on those desires. In that sense, there's an inherent randomness to our lives caused in large part by the constant and ever-changing effects of the Free Will of those many minds.

That is just a fact.

And moreover, would we want it any other way? I don't think so. Wouldn't we each rather have our individual Free Will to make our own choices in life? Rather than live in a universe where everything we think, say and do is controlled by some puppeteer we can't see?

Absolutely yes. I think we would all agree to that.

Well, then that comes with consequences. And the randomness in life, i.e., the *lack of full control* of everything that happens in our lives is part of those consequences.

NO REWARDS & NO PUNISHMENTS

No one is rewarded structurally — maybe psychologically, individually and internally — yes, sometimes — but not externally by "the Universe." And no one is structurally, externally *punished* by the universe. Said another way: there is no structural place or system of punishment that exists in the system of the universe. It only exists in the minds of some people who choose to believe in that. But that is belief-based. Not based in the structure of reality.

Yes, no exceptions.

Not even a universal structural punishment for Hitler, Stalin, Idi Amin, or Genghis Khan. They're only held accountable by themselves and that's only if they choose to be. That's what I mean by internally, individually and psychologically.

It's between Genghis Khan and Genghis Khan to figure out his stuff, if he wants to. No external structure in the universe is making him be accountable.

Now, what about consequences to Genghis Khan's actions?

Did he cause trauma and piss off the many women he raped and abused? Absolutely. Did they "deserve" what he did to them due to some "past karma"? No. Are there consequences for his actions? Absolutely yes. But it's his choice to work out those relationships in subsequent lifetimes or not. And it's also those women's choices to work out their relationships (if you want to call them that...) with him and within themselves — or not. Can those women hold him accountable in whatever way they want if they run into him in a future lifetime? Absolutely yes. All of them have their individual Free Will operating. Always.

(For what would drive such a personality to acknowledge his accountability, see my essay on "Transcending Cruelty.")

FINAL THOUGHTS

As we have said, there is no karmic "external accounting system" at play.

After the initial theory of karma was conjured up about 10,000 years ago, that idea was then added to — and conflated by others — in the thousands of years that followed. And today, the spiritual leaders on the Other Side who were the original creators of the Theory of Karma are letting it be known publicly through many individuals worldwide that those theories (karma and dharma) are now seen as being harmful, and should be discarded.

I hope that helps free you up to enjoy life now with less fear. Discernment and awareness of the consequences of one's actions is always good — yes — but now we should do the discernment with much less fear. That is the current goal of those who originally created the theory 10,000 years ago.

Instead, it is now being replaced in favor of Free Will, the idea that life is an eternal democracy, and that we can transcend cruelty.

Ego & God

Jesus did perform miracles.

However, they were only "miracles" because his ability to transform what most people consider physical reality into something less material and more energetic was "miraculous." Water into wine. Five loaves and two fish to feed thousands.

Those are the flashy miracles that most people remembered and wrote about.

But the greatest miracle he performed was the teaching of principles that prompted self-empowerment. Not slavery or subservience. He was all about teaching each of us to be self-sufficient. Not dependent on him — whether he was with us in physical form, or in spirit after he died.

He wanted each of us to live that miracle in daily life. To embody it. To demonstrate it. And he asked each of us to teach others how to do it in their daily lives. That was the task he left with us to continue.

BELIEF ONLY

This message from Jesus of self-empowerment has been lost for 2,000 years.

It was usurped by the easier "believe in Him only" message taught by Paul and many others. That all you had to do was believe in God or Jesus (or Krishna or Buddha or your guru) and all your desires would be realized. It was a simple message and an emotionally attractive message — one that many could easily get their minds and hearts around without much thinking or effort.

But, how real, how honest has this message been? How beneficial has it been for humanity? Has it promoted Jesus's desire of empowering humanity to be stronger, wiser, more self-sufficient — and happier?

Let's look at this more closely...

CENTER OF THE UNIVERSE

Thinking that God does everything for you — provides you with miracles, justice and forgiveness, with wins and successes, with riches whether material or spiritual — these are all examples of our spiritual insecurity. And of our hubris. For hubris — excessive pride or egotism — is borne out of insecurity.

Any so-called 21st century "spiritual teacher" who still preaches those sorts of messages is singing the same song that has been sung since the dawn of mankind on Earth. And by spiritual teacher, they need not be a member of a clergy. I consider anyone who promotes a value system to others to help them along life's path a "spiritual teacher." So, that could include motivational speakers, coaches of all kinds, or the author of the latest self-help book.

It is the all too alluring "song" that sounds so sweet to our ears because it tells us that we are the "center of the universe." That all roads lead through us. All miracles, all justice, all wins and successes lead through us. And to prove that is true, the spiritual teacher tells us that even God smiles on us and supports each of us (at the exclusion of others), that God delivers those miracles to each of us...if we would only believe that is true. That's all it takes. Belief.

So, if we truly analyze the underlying thinking, those spiritual teachers are telling us that even God considers us the center of the universe — because God puts each of us first...as long as we believe. No wonder it makes us feel so good!

Really?

If there is a God, would he or she be so bored or lacking in creativity or self esteem to be the superintendent of a universe in which he or she controlled all our actions? That it is all a "big game" that God is playing and only God knows the rules? That his or her ego would be so fragile that it needed us to believe *in him or her*? Or that God would set things up where the concept of forgiveness (which implies judgment) would even exist?

How boring and petty a mind that would be to supervise such a system!

I know, I know...but it "feels" so good. It feels comforting and reassuring to think we are the centers of the universe...doesn't it?

And *if God* puts each of us at the center of the universe, how good does that feel? How important does that make us feel in his eyes?

But...does it even make sense to put each of us at the center of the universe? How is that even possible?

How about trying this on for size — what if each of us were the center of *our own* universes? Let's look at that idea more closely...

"CENTER OF THE UNIVERSE" VERSUS "SELF-INTEREST"

I suggest that it is appropriate that we think of ourselves in what some might call a "self-interested" way. But unlike many others, I don't consider that a bad thing. It's not an unsavory trait. It's not lacking in spirituality, nor is it lacking in caring for our fellow humanity.

It's the truth. It's reality.

Acting in our own self-interest is what we all do, all the time. How "good" the actions that come out of that behavior are determined by how connected we are within ourselves, how well we "know ourselves." And the more self-aware we are, the more likely we will do things that make us happy. And the more we do that, the less likely we will do things that make others around us and in our community (however large we want to define it) unhappy. Because what happy person in their right mind would want to surround him or herself with unhappy miserable people?

So, we each have choices to make in life. And I maintain that it is not "being self-interested" that is bad. In fact, I think it is inherent in life. But instead, it is our lack of self-awareness, our lack of knowing who we are, of what "makes us tick" — that is what is "bad," what is lacking.

Because ultimately, how we choose to live our lives — through the various decisions we make in life — determines our level of happiness.

Reclaiming the awareness of that power we all have always had — reclaiming them from spiritual teachers who might prefer that we relinquish that power to divine beings whom they claim are "greater" than we are — is our birthright and how we can truly honor ourselves.

For millennia we have been told, arguably brainwashed, that we are "lesser," that we need to find "the divine" within us or even outside of us, that we need to believe in that, and that's all we need to do.

Looking at human history, so far that formula is not working. At least not in the past 10,000 years. The divine is not "within us" or "outside of us." There is no need to call anything "divine" if we truly "know ourselves" in the way Jesus and other great teachers have encouraged us to.

When we think and feel ourselves as "bigger than ourselves" — experiencing the vastness of our individual consciousnesses — we don't need to make that all-too-automatic jump to defining that experience as "divine." Instead, perhaps we might realize that "it" is actually us — just a different experience of ourselves than we have been used to experiencing.

Our minds are bigger than we realize. Much bigger. And that

realization is the miracle that all great teachers have encouraged us to see — and to live.

By coming to that realization, I think we'll also find greater freedom and inner peace in recognizing our own individual place in the universe. That each of us has. That each of us has always had, and will always have.

And not at the center of the universe. But instead, wherever we are.

God — Pettiness, Fear & Punishment

L et's assume God exists. Let's also assume — as believers believe — that He, She or It is smarter than we are (or as some believe, omniscient or all knowing) and is all loving.

[For the rest of this essay, I will use the lower case and masculine form, to make the essay easier to read, but you may assume that it includes He, She, or It.]

PETTINESS

So if he is smarter than we are, then we should begin by removing all petty behavior from his behavior, that people have attributed to him.

By "petty" I mean the type of thinking that is based on narrow thinking.

But you don't have to think of it as "petty." Think of it as "inconsistent with the type of thinking that a supreme being would have."

So, for example, a supreme being would not want to tell people what to do all the time. That would be petty behavior. It would essentially be like saying, "God enjoys being a slaveowner" (i.e., controlling people, making them do things they don't want to do, ordering them around, etc.).

Really? Does that make sense?

Is a slaveowner mentality consistent with what you would consider a supremely intelligent, loving being?

Telling people what to do and controlling their behavior would also be a very boring job. And we must assume that he's smarter than picking a job like that, if in fact he's omniscient.

After all, most *human beings* would not pick a job like that because of all the drawbacks associated with it, so why would an "omniscient being" pick that job? We must assume that he's at least as smart as most human beings, right?

Oh, and while we're on the subject of "petty" thinking, let's get this one out of the way…God and sports betting…

Nor do I think God bets on sports teams…or favors or influences the outcomes of games. So, all those prayers and thanks to "the Lord" for winning the game, are falling on deaf ears — it simply is not behavior consistent with an entity who is "all knowing" (or at least is smarter than we are) and "all loving." I mean "picking sides"…really? C'mon man. Now, if you're asking your dead grandfather for help, that would make sense to me — dead relatives and friends can definitely be partial! But, God?

FEAR

What about fear? Is that the type of emotion an "all loving" God would want to spread among his people?

I don't think so.

Instead, I think he would want us to live *our own* lives, make our own choices based on Free Will and enjoy our lives as fully as possible *without fear* because fear *limits* our level of happiness.

Ask yourself — why would a parent want his or her children to be miserable and live in fear? (I know, I know…there are parents out there who are terrible parents like that, but remember, we're talking about God here, not just ANY parent…)

Fear *contracts* us, it *limits* us, it *drains* our energy. All of that is inconsistent with what promotes happiness.

So if we assume that God is all loving, we must assume that he would want us to be happy. And therefore he would not be an entity that spreads fear or would want to have fear created *in us*.

And so anyone who says that "fear is important" is not speaking from God's standpoint — but instead from the human standpoint of desiring *to control* other human beings.

All of that is already known by human beings, i.e., the effect of fear on behavior. Ask any human psychologist.

So again, if one assumes that God is omniscient, then he *must* at least be smarter than all of those humans who *already know* the effect of fear. It is well researched, and one must assume that God already knows about that research — otherwise he would not be omniscient and, moreover, would not be an entity anyone would want to believe in.

PUNISHMENT

The same thinking about God applies to the issue of punishment.

It does not make sense that God would be a being who punishes, knowing that it would create *more* misery in the person, which would in turn lead to *more and more* miserable people in the world. That would, as we have seen in other essays, lead to more cruel behavior.

And God would also not use punishment as a method to *change behavior.*

All the behavioral research indicates that punishment does not change behavior, so why would an all loving God punish people? Assuming he's omniscient, he would know *at least as much* as human beings know about punishment. And it is well known that punishment does *not* change behavior.

In fact, recently I was in Los Angeles at a breakfast meeting, and the Los Angeles County district attorney spoke about punishment not working in the criminal justice system — that 64% (2 out of 3) of everyone who is jailed, once released, goes back to jail within 6 months and one third of that group are back in jail within 3 weeks. Similar statistics exist nationwide.

FINAL THOUGHTS

If you choose to believe in God, you should sleep deeply knowing that God loves you, will not punish you, wants *you* to make *your own* decisions about your life, supports you in *all* decisions that you make, and is *not* judging you.

I hope this helps you live your life freer from fear — with more energy and enjoyment.

Experiencing Eternity?

Have you ever wondered if it's possible?
Have you ever wondered what it's like?

This experience has been debated, pondered, interpreted, dismissed, and embraced by hundreds of millions of people over the millennia.

I'd like to discuss this with you now, maybe in a little bit of a different way than you're normally accustomed to.

One common way of describing an experience that has often been interpreted as "eternity" or "oneness"...

I was standing in the sand dunes at the beach at sunset. The horizon began to shimmer. Then suddenly everything changed in a way I had never experienced before. The sparkle of the sun on the water seemed to transport me to a different state of consciousness. I wasn't just seeing with my eyes – I was perceiving everything around me. I was seeing, sensing, becoming, being the sand, the waves, the endless many-hued sky. My body was still standing on the dunes, but I can't say "I" was standing because suddenly "I" was all energy, and everything around me was all the same energy, flowing within me and without me (almost as if I was George Harrison...). What I normally thought of as solid matter was now a seamless reflection of all this golden light energy. My body seemed to melt away. I became "one" with the sand and surf – and then, for a moment, with all of creation. I felt tremendously expanded and alive. Joy and relief filled my mind as I finally understood that I was a part of something greater.

Poets like T.S. Eliot and William Blake, philosophers like

Plato and Aristotle, spiritual leaders like the Dalai Lama and the Pope, and even comedians like Woody Allen ("Eternity is really long, especially near the end...") have all given their perspective on this sort of experience.

The usual reaction and interpretation of this experience is to immediately jump to the conclusion that it describes our connection with something greater than us, something that is "not us." That's the most common reaction. Oneness with God, the Universe, Nature, or some divine creation.

But does that make sense?

Simply by looking at the description above, what is the common denominator? Clearly, it is "I." The constant throughout the experience is that *he* is describing it, and is conscious and aware throughout the entire experience. Otherwise, how would he be able to describe it?

Yes, it may be true that he is not experiencing in the usual way he is used to experiencing "being awake." He is not experiencing the usual analysis of and focus on the minutia of what is going on in his immediate environment, his body, and the active analytical part of his mind — sometimes probably overly analytical part of his mind — however, obviously his mind is *still awake and active.* The analytical part of his mind is also still awake, functioning and active, otherwise he would not be able to draw the distinctions he so clearly does in his description of this experience.

I think people often misinterpret the experience of "melting away" — of less awareness of the body — as a merging with something else. With a "oneness."

But if there is self-awareness, even a different type of self-awareness, is that actually oneness?

A GOOD NIGHT'S SLEEP

What if we looked at this differently?

What if we look at ourselves first? And what if in looking at ourselves, we accept that our experience can sometimes be different from what it usually is — that we do experience *differences in our experiences* all the time. This happens frequently throughout our lives, doesn't it?

For example, if you have a really good night's sleep, you wake up incredibly refreshed, and when you walk outside and you look at the leaves on the trees, it's as if you can see like you've never seen before — you see the details of what makes up the leaves in a way that you have never noticed before. All the details may become clearer to your vision and you may even feel "more connected" with the leaf as you become less aware of your body (perhaps because your body is so incredibly refreshed and not therefore requiring so much of your attention).

At least your experience of the leaf seems that way. However, does that mean you have "become one with the leaf," that you have lost your individuality in the process of seeing the leaf in this new way because you got an incredibly good night's sleep and are unusually refreshed — and have lost your body awareness and now feel "connected with the leaf"?

I think not.

You are not "one with the leaf"…you and the leaf are still separate. It just *feels* that way because you feel more connected with the leaf. But why do you feel connected? You feel connected because you are more connected *within yourself*, within your mind — if there is any experience of "oneness"…

it is with yourself.

That is profound and sublime all at the same time, and as such, you should acknowledge it and embrace it. But instead, the most common reaction is to project that connectedness externally to the world around you.

Why do we do that?

I think we do it for a number reasons, some are institutional and some are internal, but in the end we have internalized it all ourselves and the responsibility is ours. I think spiritual institutions have told us for millennia that we are not worthy, that those institutions are the only vehicles through which we can experience greatness, through which we can experience something larger than our normal sense of self. But, in the end, it's our responsibility for having "bought" that line of thinking.

Instead, I think there can be a different interpretation of this experience...

THE SAME "YOU" BUT DIFFERENT

It is the same "you," except a different "you" at the same time.

Maybe more accurately, it is the same "you" experiencing your world around you in a different way because *you are different*, not the world. And it's not even your "relationship" with your world that is different. It is all you. It is the experiencer which is you, your mind, your consciousness, your awareness, whatever you want to call it...which is "experiencing itself" *in a different way*. It is experiencing itself in this case in a more refreshed, clearer way than usual, which then causes the experience of the leaf to appear to be different.

Now, let's look at this experience in the sand dunes through that lens.

What if his mind has simply started to experience aspects of itself that he is generally unfamiliar with, and now is just beginning to explore? (If it's a brand new experience, the "newness" of it alone will be powerful and almost overwhelming initially.)

What if sitting in the dunes and being in that quiet moment somehow was a catalyst and stimulated his neurophysiology to start to experience in this different way. In other words, I think it's always a combination of mind, body, emotions, overall energy — the whole package in other words — that is responsible for any experience on a moment to moment basis in life. And as such, since that combination is always in flux, our experiences are always changing — even the experience of the same thing is never exactly the same.

And so, it's no different if you were like this guy who was standing in the dunes. In my opinion, he could just as well have had the experience elsewhere, and maybe some of you have had such a similar experience, for example sitting in your cubicle at work. In other words, there is no magic to the setting, to the external environment — nothing magical that needs to be there. I think any individual's nervous system — that is, whatever state their neurophysiology is in at the time — could elicit this type of experience.

But, now that we've narrowed it down to "ourselves experiencing ourselves in a very different way" that may be causing us to feel "blown away" by a new sense of time, expansion, and connectedness — in this case while he's standing in the sand dunes just south of Pismo Beach — what about this "experience of eternity"?

ARE WE EXPERIENCING "ETERNITY"?

So, let's look more closely at what we have so far been loosely referring to as "the experience." Is it actually the experience of "eternity"?

First, let's talk about "Time." What is "time"? Time is defined as *"the measurement of the continuum of change."* That said, how we measure time itself is somewhat arbitrary — we humans make up the metrics. Makes sense, right?

Have you ever been asked by an inquisitive young child, "Who decided that a day was 24 hours long? Or, why does a year have 12 months in it? Or, how come a lunar year is different?"

And so forth. These are all arbitrary measurements that we have created in our attempt to organize our lives less chaotically. Those metrics are human-made.

Plus, we all subjectively experience time differently. Sometimes the same work day seems like it drags on for much longer than usual if not much is going on. And, other times the day just speeds by, and the next thing you know, it's dinner time! How many of you have experienced not knowing what time or day it is when you are on vacation? Exactly. See what I mean?

Our sense of time can vary. Our subjective experience of it can be different.

Now, what is "Eternity?" First, it must be *not influenced* by "time."

And remember, since "time" is the measurement of the continuum of change, the concept of eternity tells us that anything that is "eternal" must be *uninfluenced by the continuum of change.*

Still with me?

Stated again: "Eternity" is whatever is *uninfluenced by* the continuum of change.

So what would fall under the category of eternity? In other words, what can we even talk about that is *uninfluenced* by the continuum of change?

How about this for starters — the existence of matter, the unchanging patterns of matter, life itself...our very existence.

But can any of those be actually *experienced*?

You see, every experience we have is *part of* that continuum of change. And if eternity exists (conceptually, not spatially) and is uninfluenced by that continuum of change, then, while we can talk about it and understand it conceptually, we can't really *directly* experience it.

So, what is going on when people report having these

experiences — in the sand dunes perhaps — which they may *interpret* as an "experience of eternity or timelessness"?

AS COMPARED TO WHAT?

I often say, "As compared to what?" Let's look at "this experience" through that lens.

Each of us human beings — compared to one another — experiences "this" differently. We always experience whatever we want to call "this experience" differently — depending on who we are. *Each person* even experiences it somewhat differently (within him or herself) at different times. There is no constant, identical experience of this or any experience.

So there really isn't a "this" — there are really a bunch of different "this's" — at least one for every mind that exists, multiplied by some unknown number — in other words, A LOT! Which essentially means there really isn't a "this."

But instead, there are many, many variations on a *somewhat similar experience.*

So, if every experience we have exists within, and therefore is influenced by, the continuum of change — and if eternity is uninfluenced by the continuum of change, then what exactly are we experiencing?

EXPERIENCE OF WHAT?

I think it's a combination of two things —

1) We are experiencing our own minds, but we are *experiencing our own minds in a very different way than it is usually experienced.* So there is a significant subjective component to these experiences.

2) And, at the same time, *we are experiencing more clearly the vastness of reality* — the myriad of energy and subtlety of that expression of energy that exists in the universe. So there is an objective component as well.

And I think it only seems, as if, "beyond time" at first because we are so unfamiliar with how diverse and unexplored (and vast) our own minds are. Not to mention how foreign our respective experience of the vastness of the universe is to each of us.

So then, I think the combination of the newness of both of those experiences tends to almost overshadow and overwhelm all previous interpretations of experience up to that point, and the individual consequently defaults to the mystical — to interpreting the experience as an "experience of eternity" (or oneness, or God, etc.).

However...

As we have discussed, it cannot be the *experience of* eternity. Eternity as a concept can only be understood and talked about...it cannot be experienced.

Could this sense of "eternity" that is being experienced be reflective of the vastness and expansiveness of our own minds? Could these experiences be hints evidencing the eternity of the mind?

And, as we said, since *all* experience occurs within the continuum of change, our experiences of the so-called eternity of our minds are also subject to change. So, while they are not actual experiences of eternity itself (a logical and experiential impossibility), they may be reminders of our individual vastness and diverseness — "dancing around" the concept of eternity.

Perhaps it is us connecting and experiencing aspects of ourselves in a way that we normally may not be accustomed to, and experiencing the world, therefore, around us in a way that we may not normally be accustomed to.

However, I think as we grow in our familiarity with "who we are" *inside*, by continuing to regularly "turn within" and experience ourselves in that more profound and different way, and as we know ourselves more fully within, these experiences (both of ourselves inside and the vastness of the universe outside) gradually become more and more familiar and eventually, become the norm. They become a normal, natural part of the fabric of our everyday life.

NOT JUST FOR "THE FEW"

And, these are not, as some spiritual traditions have claimed, experiences only available to a few. These are not experiences that are only available to people who are experienced long-term meditators, spiritual seekers or ascetics in a monastery or an ashram.

No.

These experiences are available to everyone, anytime. And if someone has their variation on such experiences and describes it to you, do not be jealous of them, because it does not mean they are more evolved or more spiritually important than you are. It simply means that their neurophysiology aligned in a certain way at that moment and created their version of the experience. Their fears subsided just enough to allow that experience to occur.

And, you can experience them as well, anytime.

We are all much bigger than we think we are. In other words, our minds are so much bigger than we think they are. There are always areas and avenues of our minds that we can explore and exercise and use that we have not yet uncovered. And by uncovering these areas of our minds, we will be able to experience and uncover for ourselves many other areas of reality that exist all around us.

Think of it this way — how much more comfortable and easy could it be than to simply allow our mind to experience itself more and more?

This is what all the great spiritual teachers, poets and seers throughout time have meant when they have said these words,

"Know thyself." By doing so, we can all experience the "eternity of ourselves" as a normal, everyday occurrence.

And that simple, intimate experience inevitably infuses us with the freedom, self-confidence and compassion that will ensure continuing happiness in our lives.

FINAL THOUGHTS

So, after all is said and done, you might ask, "Who cares"? Outside of a few philosophers and academics who are into esoteric bantering about of ideas and abstract concepts?

I am a practical guy. So, I look at this whole discussion from its potential practical value for us as individuals — and for us as a world community.

For me, it is important to "demystify the mystical." To get greater clarification and understanding — about this whole supposed experience of eternity and notion of "oneness" with creation — because when we realize that there is no ONE way it is experienced, that in fact it cannot literally be experienced at all, and that we all can have *many* experiences of this "altered state" (sometimes referred to as an experience of eternity), it can actually bring us *closer together as a world community.*

Because it dispenses with the notion that there is ONE way that is THE way.

So, when we realize this, we can stop wasting our time seeking that illusory goal. And we can stop lording ourselves over others, claiming to have THE way, trying to make ourselves "more important" than others. Not just in the spiritual realm, but also in politics, business, and our everyday lives.

I actually think that a clearer — more down-to-earth — understanding of this whole area of metaphysics might not only expand our inner knowledge of ourselves, but could also be the seeds for a more peaceful world.

About the Foundation

The "Turning Within" Meditation and Overcoming the Fear of Death Foundations are nonprofit 501(c)(3) organizations located in Hawthorne, California and are qualified under U.S. federal law by the IRS. Their mission is to help people, regardless of their belief system, reduce their anxiety, and overcome their fear of death and related fears, so they can free up that energy to live more productive, enjoyable lives.

Donations to support the Foundations' work around the world can be made via their websites at:

www.TurningWithin.org
www.OvercomingTheFearOfDeath.org

Donations are tax deductible to the extent allowed by the IRS.

The Foundations also have FaceBook pages at:
www.facebook.com/TurningWithin.org
www.facebook.com/OvercomingTheFearOfDeath

About the Author

Kelvin H. Chin is the Executive Director and Founder of both the Overcoming the Fear of Death Foundation and the nonprofit TurningWithin.org. Working with audiences on death and dying issues since the 1980s, Kelvin has taught numerous seminars for the healthcare industry, was a state-certified Long Term Care Ombudsman for the California Department of Aging, and a co-founder of the Center For Medical Ethics and Mediation.

Bringing greater clarity to his client's thinking in their personal and business life is something Kelvin has applied throughout his 40-year career, including teaching meditation worldwide to more than 5,000 people since the 1970s in schools, businesses, the U.S. Army and at West Point. Kelvin also formerly held CMO roles at AmLaw100 law firms, and was a VP for the American Arbitration Association.

Kelvin was born in Boston, raised in Norwood, Massachusetts, and has since lived and worked in 7 countries. He has delivered more than 2,000 presentations with clients in 45 countries. While at Dartmouth College, he studied at the Université de Strasbourg, France. He is a graduate of Dartmouth, Yale Graduate School and Boston College Law School, and is the father of two artistically talented children.

Kelvin can be contacted at
www.KelvinChin.org
and followed on
Twitter @KelvinHChin
Instagram @kelvin.h.chin
Facebook kelvin.chin1

Subscribe to his YouTube channel
youtube.com/c/KelvinChinTurningWithin

HOW TO GIFT THIS BOOK
To a Friend or a Loved One…

To get a copy of this book mailed to your home,
or to get an e-book downloaded now…

HERE'S HOW...
Go to this Link:
https://www.kelvinhenrychin.com/